COMPREHENSIVE RESEARCH
AND STUDY GUIDE

William
Blake

EDITED AND WITH AN INTRODUCTION
BY HAROLD BLOOM

CURRENTLY AVAILABLE

BLOOM'S MAJOR DRAMATISTS	BLOOM'S MAJOR NOVELISTS	BLOOM'S MAJOR POETS	BLOOM'S MAJOR SHORT STORY WRITERS
Aeschylus	Jane Austen	Maya Angelou	Jorge Luis Borges
Aristophanes	The Brontës	Elizabeth Bishop	Italo Calvino
Bertolt Brecht	Willa Cather	William Blake	Raymond Carver
Anton Chekhov	Stephen Crane	Gwendolyn Brooks	Anton Chekhov
Henrik Ibsen	Charles Dickens	Robert Browning	Joseph Conrad
Ben Johnson	William Faulkner	Geoffrey Chaucer	Stephen Crane
Christopher Marlowe	F. Scott Fitzgerald	Sameul Taylor Coleridge	William Faulkner
Arthur Miller	Nathaniel Hawthorne	Dante	F. Scott Fitzgerald
Eugene O'Neill	Ernest Hemingway	Emily Dickinson	Nathaniel Hawthorne
Shakespeare's Comedies	Henry James	John Donne	Ernest Hemingway
Shakespeare's Histories	James Joyce	H.D.	O. Henry
Shakespeare's Romances	D. H. Lawrence	T. S. Eliot	Shirley Jackson
Shakespeare's Tragedies	Toni Morrison	Robert Frost	Henry James
George Bernard Shaw	John Steinbeck	Seamus Heaney	James Joyce
Neil Simon	Stendhal	Homer	Franz Kafka
Oscar Wilde	Leo Tolstoy	Langston Hughes	D.H. Lawrence
Tennessee Williams	Mark Twain	John Keats	Jack London
August Wilson	Alice Walker	John Milton	Thomas Mann
	Edith Wharton	Sylvia Plath	Herman Melville
	Virginia Woolf	Edgar Allan Poe	Flannery O'Connor
		Poets of World War I	Edgar Allan Poe
		Shakespeare's Poems & Sonnets	Katherine Anne Porter
		Percy Shelley	J. D. Salinger
		Alfred, Lord Tennyson	John Steinbeck
		Walt Whitman	Mark Twain
		William Carlos Williams	John Updike
		William Wordsworth	Eudora Welty
		William Butler Yeats	

William Blake

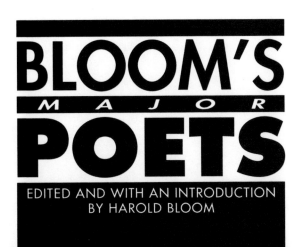

BLOOM'S *MAJOR* POETS

EDITED AND WITH AN INTRODUCTION
BY HAROLD BLOOM

First Printing
1 3 5 7 9 8 6 4 2

Library of Congress Cataloging-in-Publication Data

William Blake / Harold Bloom, ed..
        p. cm. — (Bloom's major poets)
Includes bibliographical references and index.
    ISBN 0-7910-6812-9
    1. Blake William, 1757–1857—Criticism and interpretation.   I.
Bloom,
Harold. II. Series.
    PR4147 .W444 2002
    821'.7—dc21

Chelsea House Publishers
1974 Sproul Road, Suite 400
Broomall, PA 19008-0914

The Chelsea House World Wide Web address is http://www.chelseahouse.com

Contributing Editor: Suzanne Barton Piorkowski

Layout by EJB Publishing Services

CONTENTS

USER'S GUIDE

This volume is designed to present biographical, critical, and bibliographical information on the author and the author's best-known or most important short stories. Following Harold Bloom's editor's note and introduction is a concise biography of the author that discusses major life events and important literary accomplishments. A plot summary of each story follows, tracing significant themes, patterns, and motifs in the work. An annotated list of characters supplies brief information on the main characters in each story. As with any study guide, it is recommended that the reader read the story beforehand, and have a copy of the story being discussed available for quick reference.

A selection of critical extracts, derived from previously published material, follows each character list. In most cases, these extracts represent the best analysis available from a number of leading critics. Because these extracts are derived from previously published material, they will include the original notations and references when available. Each extract is cited, and readers are encouraged to check the original publication as they continue their research. A bibliography of the author's writings, a list of additional books and articles on the author and their work, and an index of themes and ideas conclude the volume.

ABOUT THE EDITOR

Harold Bloom is Sterling Professor of the Humanities at Yale University and Henry W. and Albert A. Berg Professor of English at the New York University Graduate School. He is the author of over 20 books, and the editor of more than 30 anthologies of literary criticism.

Professor Bloom's works include *Shelly's Mythmaking* (1959), *The Visionary Company* (1961), *Blake's Apocalypse* (1963), *Yeats* (1970), *A Map of Misreading* (1975), *Kabbalah and Criticism* (1975), *Agon: Toward a Theory of Revisionism* (1982), *The American Religion* (1992), *The Western Canon* (1994), and *Omens of Millennium: The Gnosis of Angels, Dreams, and Resurrection* (1996). *The Anxiety of Influence* (1973) sets forth Professor Bloom's provocative theory of the literary relationships between the great writers and their predecessors. His most recent books include *Shakespeare: The Invention of the Human*, a 1998 National Book Award finalist, *How to Read and Why* (2000), and *Stories and Poems for Extremely Intelligent Children of All Ages* (2001).

Professor Bloom earned his Ph.D. from Yale University in 1955 and has served on the Yale faculty since then. He is a 1985 MacArthur Foundation Award recipient and served as the Charles Eliot Norton Professor of Poetry at Harvard University in 1987–88. In 1999 he was awarded the prestigious American Academy of Arts and Letters Gold Medal for Criticism. Professor Bloom is the editor of several other Chelsea House series in literary criticism, including BLOOM'S MAJOR SHORT STORY WRITERS, BLOOM'S MAJOR NOVELISTS, BLOOM'S MAJOR DRAMATISTS, MODERN CRITICAL INTERPRETATIONS, MODERN CRITICAL VIEWS, and BLOOM'S BIOCRITIQUES.

EDITOR'S NOTE

My Introduction leaps forward to Blake's final phase, so as to round off this little volume.

On "The Tyger" I particularly admire Martin Price's balancings of terror and symmetry, while I find David Erdman illuminates the historical background of "London" better than anyone else could do.

"The Mental Traveller" is viewed by Northrop Frye as an ironic vision of Blake's Orc cycle, after which John Sutherland further adumbrates the poem's complexities.

"The Crystal Cabinet" is studied as a mythic text by Irene Chayes and as alchemy by Kathleen Raine.

I analyze the "Contraries" of "The Marriage of Heaven and Hell", and W.J.T. Mitchell and the great Victorian poet Swinburne sensitively examine the rhetorical splendors of Blake's wonderful prose poem.

Harold Bloom

After *Jerusalem*, Blake wrote very little poetry, and devoted himself to his work as painter and engraver. The most considerable poem left in manuscript from his later years is *The Everlasting Gospel*, a series of notebook fragments on the theme of the necessity for the forgiveness of sins. There are powerful passages among these fragments, but they do not add anything to *Jerusalem* as imaginative thought, and Blake did not bother to arrange them in any definite form. The rhetorical directness of some of the fragments has made them popular, but their very freedom from the inventiveness of Blake's mythmaking has the effect of rendering them poetically uninteresting.

This is not true of Blake's last engraved poem, "The Ghost of Abel", a dramatic scene composed in 1822 as a reply to Byron's drama *Cain*. Byron's Cain fights free of natural religion and its fears only to succumb to a murderous dialectic by which every spiritual emancipation of a gifted individual is paid for through alienation from his brethren, the consequence being that a dissenter from the orthodoxy of negations in moral values is compelled to become an unwary Satanist. Blake's very subtle point is that the covenant of Christ, as he interprets it, takes man beyond the "cloven fiction" of moral good and moral evil, the "hateful siege of contraries" experienced by Milton's Satan on Mount Niphates, and into the clarification of seeing that only a part of what is called moral good is actually good to the imagination of real life of man. Vengeance and every similar mode of hindering another can have no part in an imaginative morality, and for Blake there is no other morality worthy of the name. *The Ghost of Abel,* which makes surprisingly effective use of Blake's long line, the fourteener, as a medium for dramatic dialog, is the true coda to Blake's poetry, rather than *The Everlasting Gospel*, for it makes explicit the moral basis of the laconic *Marriage of Heaven and Hell.*

At about the time he wrote *The Everlasting Gospel*, Blake re-engraved a little emblem-book, *The Gates of Paradise*, which he had first engraved as early as 1793, adding a number of rhymed couplets and an epilogue in two quatrains to the engravings and their inscriptions. The Gates of Paradise are "Mutual Forgiveness of each Vice", and the story told in epilogue is something rarer, an address "To the Accuser who is the God of This World", and one of Blake's most perfect short poems:

> Truly, My Satan, thou art but a Dunce,
> And dost not know the Garment from the Man.
> Every Harlot was a Virgin once,
> Nor can'st thou ever change Kate into Nan.
>
> Tho' thou are Worship'd by the Names Divine
> Of Jesus & Jehovah, thou art still
> The Son of Morn in weary Night's decline,
> The lost Traveller's Dream under the Hill.

The tone of this is unique in Blake, and I have not found the equivalent in any other poet. There is enormous irony here, mitigated by a gentle and mocking pity for the great antagonist, the Satan adored as Jesus and Jehovah by the religious of this world. Blake is past argument here; he has gone beyond prophetic anger and apocalyptic impatience. The Accuser is everywhere and at all times apparently triumphant, yet he is a delusion and so but a dunce. He cannot distinguish the phenomenal garment from the Real Man, the Imagination, and his spouse Rahab is only a delusion also.

States change; individuals endure. The god of the churches is still that light-bearer, son of the morning, who fell, and he is now in his weary night's decline as history moves to a judging climax. The vision of a restored man, Blake's vision, is the clear sight of a Mental Traveller in the open world of poetry. The Accuser is the dream of a lost traveler in the phenomenal world, but Blake has found his way home, and need not dream.

William Blake

Poet, artist, and engraver William Blake was born in London on November 28, 1757, the second or third child born to James Blake, a hosiery merchant, and Catherine Hermitage, whose first husband had left to her a similar business. The couple had united their enterprises with their lives in Westminster in October of 1752.

Blake was raised in his parents' home, above their business at Broad and Marshall Streets. It was an area where many merchants and tradesmen did business. The faith of his parents is uncertain; they were Christian—they were married in one Anglican church and baptized most or all of their children in another—but they did not always quite follow the Anglican or the Catholic Church. Politically, Catherine and John Blake held radical views, and the influence of this early radicalism would manifest itself throughout Blake's work. Blake's personal relationships with his family are obscure. He seems to have felt great affection for his youngest brother, Robert, and he referred to another brother, John, as "the evil one"; apparently, Blake believed his parents favored John. Still, it seems his parents did encourage the young artist: His mother hung Blake's drawings and verses in her chambers, and his father bought engravings and plaster casts for Blake to study. In any case, Blake would later discount his parents' influence on his life or work.

Blake learned the basics of reading and writing in school. When he was ten, his parents sent him to study drawing with Henry Pars (or Pars) of the Strand—whose establishment was one of London's best art schools. In the next five years, he gained a background in art history and many skills. On his own he was a great reader, reading avidly the Bible, Greek classics, and the works of Milton and Shakespeare. He was writing as early as 1767 or 1768, when he began what would become his *Poetical Sketches*.

Blake's schooling in art finally became too costly for his parents to support, and in 1771 he was apprenticed to engraver James Basire of Lincoln's Inn Fields, whose assignments to sketch Westminster Abbey may mark the first stirrings of Blake's later Gothic tendencies. His first engraving, "Joseph of Arimathea Among the

Rocks of Albion", dates to 1773, and "The Body of Edward I in His Coffin" followed a year later. When he finished his apprenticeship after years, he did not join the Stationers' Guild, which was the usual path to professional engraving; instead, he applied to the Royal Academy of Arts, into which he was accepted, in 1779, as an engraver. He studied and exhibited his engravings and watercolors there for several somewhat spotty years, despite an intense dislike of the Academy's head; to 1779 date "Edward and Eleanor," "Penance of Jane Shore in St. Paul's Church," and "Lear and Cordelia in Prison." One year after starting his studies, he completed his first project as a professional engraver and began to earn a living in the trade, working for Joseph Johnson, a purveyor of subversive literature.

In 1782, at the age of 25, he married Catherine Boucher, the daughter of a vegetable farmer. Blake taught her to read and write, and she would later assist him in his work; it is to her, too, that criticism owes the salvation of Blake's original manuscripts, for the poet felt that once his work had been published there was no need to keep its raw materials. Their marriage would last some 45 years but produce no children.

In this period, Blake began to associate with a circle of London intellectuals that included Mary Wollstonecraft, Thomas Paine, sculptor and draftsman John Flaxman, William Godwin, Rev. Anthony S. and Harriet Mathew (through Flaxman), and painters Thomas Stothard and Henri Fuseli. Mathew and his wife in particular became Blake's artistic allies; he was the center of attention at entertainments in their home, and it was Harriet Mathew and Flaxman who funded the publication of 50 copies of Blake's first book of poetry. This book, *Poetical Sketches*, containing the work of some 16 years, was released in 1783. Throughout this period, he continued to create and to exhibit artwork on both religious and secular themes; in 1784, he wrote *An Island in the Moon*, satirizing his progressive friends of the Joseph Johnson circle. Also in 1784, with friend and fellow apprentice James Parker, Blake opened his own print shop; this would eventually enable him to publish his own poetry. He developed his technique of "illuminated printing": he engraved words and artwork on copper plates and, having made the ink himself, printed his work onto paper.

Catherine was in the habit of sewing covers onto the printed books. Each illustration would be colored by hand. This was a very time-consuming process and limited the number of copies Blake could produce and thus his income and audience.

Blake supported himself and his wife through engraving by his own process and through providing engraved illustrations on commission; the latter projects resulted in connections between Blake and many radical thinkers of the 18th century. Beginning in 1789, Blake experienced a period of great literary activity, producing *Songs of Innocence* (1789), *The Book of Thel* (1789), *Tiriel* (1789), *The Marriage of Heaven and Hell* (early 1790s), and *Songs of Experience* (1794). It was in the same year, 1789, that the French Revolution began; that uprising and the American Revolution of a decade before influenced Blake's work and thought extensively.

Throughout Blake's work and literary life are allusions to spiritual concerns; indeed these, combined with the sensibilities of a political radical, inform much of his work. "I write when commanded by the spirits," he once said to a friend, "and the moment I have written I see the words fly about the room in all directions." Visions had been part of Blake's lonely childhood as early as his fifth year. Walking the streets of London, he had experienced them elaborately: a tree at Peckham Rye filled with angels, men at work in a field with angels. Blake was not the only member of his family with a clairvoyance of this sort. His older brother James claimed to see Moses and Abraham. The Blake parents did not support the visions; Catherine Blake beat young William once for describing what he saw, and on at least one other occasion his father threatened the same. Still, Blake's clairvoyance extended into his adulthood: he claimed to have seen the spirit of his brother Robert, with whom he had always had a close relationship, leap from Robert's body at the moment of death. Indeed, it was Robert's spirit, Blake said, that had described to him the process of illuminated printing. In any case, it was shortly after this experience that Blake discovered the writings of Emmanuel Swedenborg.

Swedenborg's Church of the New Jerusalem, preaching a gentle, mystical interpretation of Christianity, had a major influence on Blake's life and work, though because Blake seems to have both exalted and satirized Swedenborg's work the nature of this influence is unclear. By even the late 1780s, Blake was producing work with religious themes: "There Is No Natural Religion" (1788), for example, and "All Religions Are One" (1788). By 1796, he had strayed far enough from orthodoxy to create the etching "Lucifer and the Pope in Hell." By the end of the 18th century, Blake was producing works of Biblical theme, especially images with overtones of mysticism and divine mystery, almost exclusively.

Blake's works of lesser distinction of the mid- to late 1790s include some biographically noteworthy political material suited to the internationally turbulent times: *America: A Prophecy* (1793) and *Visions of the Daughters of Albion* (1793), *The Song of Los* (1795) and *The Four Zoas* (1795, originally entitled *Vala*). Between 1800 and 1803, Blake and Catherine lived in the seaside town of Felpham in Sussex, southern England, under the patronage of William Hayley, for whom Blake would work on a number of paintings and engravings; and it was then that Blake's political views had a direct effect on his freedom. While living there, he violently expelled an inebriated soldier, one John Scofield or Scolfield, from his garden and spoke some ill-advised words concerning the King and England's state of military preparedness. He soon was charged with sedition, and he was tried in 1803. It was around the time of his acquittal in 1804 that he began one of his best-known and most important works, the two-volume poem *Milton*, both inspired by and based largely on Milton's *Paradise Lost*; the year 1805, too, saw the publication of Macpherson's scurrilous Ossian poems—a collection of verse purported to be by a Celtic bard—for which Blake developed a passion. *Milton* was composed and etched through 1805 and the following three years.

In 1809, Blake held an exhibition of his paintings at a brother's house, hoping the event would publicize his work. It was not very well attended, and it may mark the beginning of the end of his creative period. The years following the exhibition were marked by failed enterprises and commercial errors and a few more works, such as *L'Allegro* (1815); the Blakes at this time have been described as "still poor still dirty," and Blake is known to have been turning out work for the Wedgwood catalogue and on commission. His most significant literary achievements of this period are *The Everlasting Gospel* (ca. 1818); *Jerusalem* (1820), his longest "prophetic" book;

and one of his best-known works of art, a 21-plate series illustrating the Book of Job that had been commissioned in the early 1820s by artist and patron John Linnell and was published in 1826. Blake also illustrated Dante's *Divine Comedy* in his later years; his last illustrated book, *The Ghost of Abel*, was written in 1821. In 1822, the Royal Academy voted to give to the Blakes the sum of £25 against their obvious poverty.

The artistic wasteland that followed the disappointing exhibition of 1809–1810 was mitigated to some extent by Blake's development of a new following: a group of young artists, including Samuel Palmer, who called themselves "The Ancients" and revered Blake and his work. The support of this group encouraged Blake's production of some imaginative work of the variety that he had wanted to produce all his life. Still, Blake died in his usual poverty, relatively unknown, on August 12, 1827, having continued his work in coloring and engraving until the time of his death. He was 69 years old. Catherine Blake was forced to borrow the money necessary for his burial, on the day before the 45th anniversary of their marriage. It would be nearly forty years before a biography would turn public attention back to Blake and a century before Blake would be appreciated and admired as an artist and poet. Now, he is considered the first, and among the greatest, of the English Romantics.

"The Tyger"

The 24 lines of "The Tyger" are often all of Blake's work with which readers become acquainted. Readers find in the verses 14 questions. This is a creative work, centered on creation: the very origin of this fearsome jungle cat. Blake captures the wildness of the beast—its burning eyes, its strength—with his words. The powerful opening verse is repeated to complete the poem.

In the first stanza, we meet "The Tyger." The luminous creature roams the forest at night. The writer is struck by the beauty, strength, and balance of the beast and questions what inspiration is behind its creation. Some scholars believe the tiger is Blake's version of the angel Lucifer. Like Lucifer, the tiger works alone and inspires thoughts of death; it also is strong and beautiful, as the Bible portrays the fallen angel.

The second stanza continues the powerful imagery, comparing the fire in the tiger's eyes and the fire used to create it, suggesting that the tiger is a reflection of the fires of Hell. Also given is the image of wings: a reinforcement of the connection between the tiger and angels—or possibly an image inspired by Greek mythology, particularly the myths of Prometheus and of Icarus.

Next, Blake poses more questions to the creator of the tiger, first pondering the two tiers of strength needed to mastermind the mighty animal: The architect who created the animal had to be physically strong to create its powerful heart and emotionally strong to stand up to the cat's intimidating form and nature. Then Blake mulls over the tiger's first fearful footsteps. Images follow that remind the reader of a blacksmith's shop. The verse turns to talk of the hammer, chain, and anvil used to forge the tiger and indicates the force needed to put the animal together.

The raw power of the tiger appears to be too much for the heavens to take. Blake describes the denial of dominance over the animal. The stars give up rather than fight for mastery of the tiger.

> When the stars threw down their spears
> And water'd heaven with their tears:

The writer then wonders if the Divine Being responsible for the tiger was pleased with the creation. He asks outright if the same being produced "The Tyger and The Lamb." This sets in contrast the gentle lamb with the wild-eyed "Tyger." To close out the poem, the first stanza is repeated:

> Tyger Tyger burning bright,
> In the forests of the night:
> What immortal hand or eye,
> Dare frame thy fearful symmetry?

The words do emphasize the beauty and strength of the animal. Seeing them again also reinforces the image of the strong animal, the night hunter, inspiring fear in all who see it. The last verse appears to be a refrain worth repeating. The reciting of these words again also strengthens the sound of the rhyme and rhythm of the work.

Blake's "Tyger" takes on a terrifying form. Brute strength and the ability to inspire fear are just two of the mighty cat's characteristics. Its creator must also have similar traits: strong shoulders to bear the responsibility of such an animal; a big heart to survive the tests of dread and fear; and a strong spirit to look into its fiery eyes and to master "The Tyger." Line by line, the tiger grows more powerful and frightening: a beast without boundaries. Yet, the speaker tries to reason with the mighty animal, asking about its creator and its opposite of the animal kingdom: the lamb. The work bears a similarity to Blake's "The Lamb", which appears, appropriately, in the "Innocence" part of the volume of poems. "The Tyger" is part of the "Experience." Did Blake believe that transformation from the gentle lamb into the powerful tiger is an integral part of maturation?

Students of Blake believe many of his writings reflect the major changes of the late 18th and early 19th centuries. For example, the revolutions: Industrial, American, and French. These changes in the economy, society, and politics changed the way people lived. Blake's tiger is strong, intimidating—a solitary, peripheral creature, independent of its shifting surroundings.

While attracted to Christianity, Blake did not subscribe to the tenets of one faith or another for very long during his life. Certainly the images of the lion and the lamb are rooted in the Bible. Perhaps Blake wishes to point out the Creator's hand in each animal and yet suggests the flames seen in the tiger's eyes are a reflection of the fires of Hell. Further still, the wings mentioned in the second verse can be compared to the wings of an angel. Is Blake reminding readers that the Divine Being who created the meek and gentle lamb, is the same who created the intimidating tiger? Or perhaps it is mankind who is responsible for the beast, creating it out of mankind's worst traits. If God created the tiger, then is this creature supposed to be everything that the Lamb is not—a relationship meant to symbolize the symbiosis between good and evil? If so, then does Blake mean evil to appear stronger and more attractive than the mild goodness of the Lamb?

It would be simplistic to state that "The Lamb" is good and "The Tyger" is evil. And it is probably not what Blake intended. "The Tyger" is experience. It is bright, energetic, and vital. It is familiar with its domain and is assertive in its environment. While the Lamb merely follows the flock, the tiger has learned from experience and is autonomous. No longer following the crowd or a single shepherd, the tiger is a hunter directly in search of satisfaction. Knowledge has given the animal its power: the intensity of it is seen in the beast's bright eyes.

There is one major discrepancy. While Blake's words describe power, the artwork that accompanies the poem paints a very different picture of "The Tyger"—a feline by no means ferocious. Some call the picture timid; was it Blake's intention to mitigate the effect of his textual work? While he describes a horrific animal, he paints a picture of a tame one. Why describe vivid colors and burning eyes and then offer the image of an animal clearly close to domestication? Further still, why pair imagery of a hammer and an anvil with an illustration of docility?

"The Tyger"

HAZARD ADAMS ON BLAKE'S SYSTEM

[Hazard Adams is a Professor Emeritus of Comparative Literature at the University of Washington. His publications include *Blake and Yeats: The Contrary Vision, William Blake: A Reading of the Shorter Poems*, and the novels *Many Pretty Toys* and *Home*. In this selection, he explains how Blake's system of writing makes the work so powerful.]

Readers have generally assumed that "The Tyger" is one of Blake's two or three greatest lyrics. For this reason, it is interesting to see that "The Tyger" most fully and particularly assimilates the whole of Blake's great system.[11] If we take as our criterion Blake's own view of what a poem should be, we discover that we have not overrated it. This leads us to suspect two things: that Blake's own standard is a reasonable one, at least insofar as the kind of poetry he wrote is concerned; and that an interpretation of Blake's shorter poems in the light of other and usually later expressions of the system is not only allowable but also perhaps imperative, if we are to understand what these poems really are. The meaning of "The Tyger" has remained a source of endless speculation; commentaries upon it have been general, fragmentary, or specialized. The excellent general approach to Blake of Frye, for example, puts us in a position to understand the poem but does not treat it in any detail. The interesting commentary of David V. Erdman, on the other hand, is limited by his special concern with Blake's politics.[12]

Here it is in the form which perhaps satisfied its author—the form in which Blake engraved it:[13]

> Tyger Tyger. burning bright, [.]
> In the forests of the night: [;]
> What immortal hand or eye. [,]
> Could frame thy fearful symmetry?

In what distant deeps or skies.
Burnt the fire of thine eyes?
On what wings dare he aspire?
What the hand, dare seize the fire?

And what shoulder, & what art,
Could twist the sinews of thy heart?
And when thy heart began to beat,
What dread hand? & what dread feet?

What the hammer? what the chain,
In what furnace was thy brain?
What the anvil? what dread grasp, [.]
Dare its deadly terrors clasp?

When the stars threw down their spears
And water'd heaven with their tears: [;]
Did he smile his work to see?
Did he who made the Lamb make thee?

Tyger Tyger burning bright,
In the forests of the night; [:]
What immortal hand or eye, [.]
Dare frame thy fearful symmetry?

"The Tyger" is a poem of rather simple form, clearly and cleanly proportioned, all of its statements contributing to a single, sustained, dramatic gesture. Read aloud, it is powerful enough to move many listeners (small children, for example) without their having much understanding of the poem beyond its literal expression of a dramatic situation. But Blake warns us that there is a great gulf between simplicity and insipidity. The total force of the poem comes not only from its immediate rhetorical power but also from its symbolical structure.

Blake's images, at first sensuous, are to continued inspection symbolic. Things which burn, even tigers perhaps, are either purifying something or being purified. In the dark of night, in a forest, a tiger's eyes would seem to burn. The tiger's striped body suggests this same conflagration. In any case, Blake is trying to establish a kind of brilliance about his image.

The tiger, on the other hand, is presented ambiguously. In spite of its natural viciousness, it seems to suggest also clarity and energy. If the reader has had prolonged experience with poetry and mythology, other associations will sharpen these ideas. He will perhaps associate the "forests of the night" with the traditional dark night or dark journey of the soul through the dens of demons and beasts. The tiger's brightness may suggest the force which the sun so often symbolizes in mythology.

NOTES

11. In the last chapter of his recent book, *The Piper and the Bard* (Detroit, 1959), pp. 277–287, published after this essay was completed, Robert F. Gleckner discusses parallels between "The Tyger" and *The Four Zoas*. He reaches some conclusions similar to my own, but he approaches them from an opposite direction, being interested primarily in how "The Tyger" as a song of experience throws light upon the later poem. My own discussion is a considerable development of some ideas originally presented in *Blake and Yeats: The Contrary Vision* (Ithaca, 1955), pp. 236–240.

12. *Blake: Prophet Against Empire* (Princeton, 1954), particularly pp. 178–181.

13. Blake's punctuation was inconsistent, particularly in his use of commas and periods, colons and semicolons. This inconsistency is made even more confusing (if that is possible) by his tendency to write commas that look like periods and semicolons that look like colons. This problem is well illustrated by the plate from *Songs of Experience* on which "The School Boy" is engraved (reproduced in Northrop Frye's Modern Library selection of Blake). In the word "nip'd" of line one, stanza five, the apostrophe looks like a period, though in "strip'd" of line three it is clearly an apostrophe. I have chosen to reproduce Blake's punctuation as best I can without being swayed by a desire for consistency. Possible alternative readings appear in the brackets. No two Blake scholars have agreed on the correct transcription; it is clear that subtleties of interpretation cannot often be based upon Blakes punctuation.

—Hazard Adams, "Reading Blake's Lyrics: 'The Tyger'," *Discussions of William Blake*, ed. John E. Grant (Boston: D.C. Heath and Company, 1961), 53–54.

JOHN E. GRANT'S QUESTIONS FOR THE READER AND WRITER

[John E. Grant taught at the University of Iowa, edited *Discussions of William Blake*, and co-edited *Blake's Visionary Forms Dramatic* with David V. Erdman. In this detailed analysis, "The Art and Argument of 'The Tyger'", Grant poses questions to both the reader and the writer.]

The reader may become wearied with tracing the nuances of doubt because Blake's own ideas are usually precise and definite. But in "The Tyger," as in such poems as "Earth's Answer," "The Little Vagabond," or the opening stanzas of "A Little Boy Lost," the speaker is not Blake. Nevertheless, in these cases the speaker is treated with sympathy and patient understanding. After having learned much of what Blake knew, a number of Blake scholars have displayed a very un-Blakean impatience with those of Blake's characters who have not achieved comparable illumination, though Blake himself had great sympathy for those like Tom Paine who were finally on the side of the "devils," no matter how much doubt and error they spread.

If we follow the poem through, interpreting it word for word and bearing Blake's heavy punctuation and powerful measured cadence, we should be able to establish a basic reading against which to test any general interpretation. Since such a reading has never really been attempted before,[6] I shall mention a number of quite obvious things.[7] The speaker begins by addressing the Tyger, and in the heavy alliteration and primarily trochaic beat of his words the beast is envisioned as burning in the darkness of nocturnal forests.[8] Flame is a clear symbol for passion[9] and is set off by the blackness of the nocturnal forests. Forests per se are sinister symbols in Blake, corresponding to Dante's *selva oscura*, for they stand for the merely or triumphantly vegetable world he elsewhere calls the "stems of vegetation" at the bottom of the state of generation. A beast whose natural home is in such a place would therefore likewise be ominous. The contrast between fire and night, of course, corresponds to the contrast of yellow and black stripes ringing the Tyger itself.

As a paraphrase for the question Blake's speaker puts to the Tyger about its origins, "What immortal made you?" is totally inadequate. Part of the force in the questioning of the first stanza derives from the fact that the fourth line is iambic. The movement from trochaic to iambic in the third line corresponds to the shift from vision to question.[10] With this in mind we can better paraphrase the import of the question itself as follows: "What immortal organ could produce (by hand) or even conceive (with the eye), shape, or limit your fearful or terrifying balance or proportion?" The grammatical possibilities are: "How in the world did he have either the ability or the courage, etc., to do it?" or "Why did he presume against the Tyger's nature—or transgress against man—to do so?" And "frame" means to form, contrive, or limit (like a picture or a prison). Idealism so pervades Blake's thought that every incarnate thing can be considered to be in a trap. Most readings seem to assume that the first alternatives for "could" and "frame" are the only relevant ones, but nothing in the poem necessitates such restricted interpretations. The speaker is too bemused to attain certainty.

Stanza two inquires first into the source of the material cause of the beast and then into the antecedent circumstances of its efficient cause or maker. We oversimplify the first question if we take it to ask whether the fire in the Tyger's eyes came from hell ("deeps") or heaven ("skies"), but this is better than Bateson's suggestion that the "deeps" are "perhaps volcanoes rather than oceans."[11] Neither of Bateson's equivalents is at all satisfactory, because the reader knows by this time that a metaphysical creature like the Tyger could never have had a merely physical place of origin. Observe, however, that "deeps or skies" does not imply traditional metaphysics and it has the exact combination of definiteness and suggestive vagueness which characterizes both the question and the questioner. The merely conceptual translation "hell or heaven" obscures the real significance implied by the question, namely, that the speaker *doesn't know*. It is also necessary to observe that the poem has moved from a concern with the creator's eye in the first stanza to that of the Tyger here, thus beginning to link the two.

The exact implication of the last two lines of the second stanza is even harder to spell out. "Did the creator go under his own power (wings) or that of another?" or "What remarkable wings would enable him—to aspire?" "Aspire" seems to mean "soar," "mount," or "tower" as in "Ah! Sun-flower" (though there a goal is indicated) to some vaguely understood place up in the "skies" where the creator could get the fire of the Tyger's eyes. But if we follow Blake's punctuation, "aspire" means aspiration for its own sake and thus it would indicate ambitious pride, a state of mind very objectionable to the orthodox, though not in the same sense to Blake. And the word "dare" can be taken to reinforce the suggestion of a dubious audacity, though it may simply imply courage. The parallel structure of the fourth line also maintains this dual ambiguity; it asks "What kind of hand would have the courage or presumption to seize (i.e., grasp decisively, or steal) the fire (which is shown in the Tyger's eyes)." It should also be observed that "dare" is probably the present subjunctive tense of the verb, a fact which tends to bring these presumably past events into the imagination's present focus as the questioner meditates on them.

The sinister overtones of the creator's actions have been scarcely regarded by criticism based on the supposition that Blake is the speaker, but there is nothing in the poem which rules them out. Since "All Religions are One," it is useful to observe parallels to the action of the poem in myth. Bateson recalls Prometheus, the fire bringer— and (co-)maker of man—who stole fire from heaven.[12] A creative blacksmith reminds us of Hephaestus. Both had trouble With Zeus, a fact which becomes relevant to "The Tyger" when we begin to ask why the creator would have to "aspire," above himself.

NOTES

6. The nearest approach to this kind of study, except for Mr. Adams' accompanying essay, is contained in Stanley Gardner, *Infinity on the Anvil* (Oxford, 1954), pp. 123–130. But even Gardner is more concerned with the resonances of the major symbols than in the poem as a developing whole.

7. A complete rhetorical analysis should be coordinated with a prosodic one and both should be combined with a semantic study. Among the things one would wish most to note is the subtle and brilliant use of the words "In" and "What" especially in the initial position of the lines which follow their first introduction in lines 2 and 3. But the coordination of this material would make this essay too complicated.

8. "Nocturnal forests" does not, indeed, properly render the overtones of "forests of the night," though it is better than the other annotational suggestion, "forests at night," given by F. W. Bateson in his edition, *Selected Poems of William Blake* (London, 1957), p. 118. (Hereafter called Bateson.) These paraphrases give priority to the forests, whereas the poem has it the other way around. We get closer to the spirit of Blake's image by recalling that Miltonic void that is "the realm of Chaos and Old Night."

9. A friend draws my attention to the adverb "bright," a word with primarily favorable overtones. But if the Tyger is partly admired for its brightness, it is seen by this speaker only as a bonfire, not as a forest fire that will burn up the forests of error.in the apocalypse. Only a Reprobate could see it in this way. For the forest fire image, see David V. Erdman, *Blake: Prophet Against Empire* (Princeton, 1954), p. 181, where Jeremiah 21: 12–14 is cited.

10. The meter of this line is remarkable, for it seems (to me, and to at least one other reader) to start out trochaic and melt into iambic. This correlates with a tendency on the reader's part to read "What" as exclamatory until he discovers in line four that it is interrogative.

11. P. 118.

12. P. 118.

—John E. Grant, "The Art and Argument of 'The Tyger'," *Discussions of William Blake*, ed. John E. Grant (Boston: D.C. Heath and Company, 1961), 66–68.

Harold Pagliaro on the Changing View of "The Tyger"

[Harold Pagliaro taught at Columbia University and was a Professor at Swarthmore College. He wrote *Henry Fielding: A Literary Life*, *Naked Heart: A Soldier's Journey to the Front*, and *Selfhood and Redemption in Blake's Songs*. In his *Selfhood and Redemption in Blake's Songs*, he offers an explanation as to why the words in "The Tyger" are so different from the artwork illustrating it.]

Clearly for him a fixed state of things has passed. In perceiving the Tyger as he has, he is compelled to define Tyger, Creator, Lamb, and himself anew, in such a way as to integrate them into a new scheme of things. If he is in any sense compelled to wonder whether the Creator of the Tyger is also the creator of the Lamb—"Did he who made the Lamb make thee?"—then one must conclude there was a time when he believed, however unconsciously, that the answer was no. One must also conclude he is at least on the verge of admitting to consciousness that Lamb, Tyger, and speaker are parts of a single system, however different they may be from each other. And in understanding this special unity of the Creator's devising, the speaker "accepts" the creation which is both deadly and loving, and he also recognizes that he himself includes the Tyger no less than the Lamb. The speaker has passed from "deadly terror" to a new knowledge of the system of things of which he is a part. This implies, equally, his passage to a new knowledge of himself.

In the final stanza, "dare" for "could" is the first gloss on this new condition; the apparently benign Tyger of the illustration is the second. "Could" in the context implies the speaker's willingness to search for the capacity to create the Tyger. "Dare" implies the knowledge that a creator is available, the remaining question having to do with the "willingness" to create it and what such willingness represents. The movement from "could" to "dare" represents no shift in objective fact, only a changed perception of the speaker. Having wondered "could?" he has come to imagine "dare!" with all it implies for the power and morality of the Creator and himself. He has acknowledged the fact that the Tyger's fearful symmetry has been framed. And in some sense he himself has framed it within the limits of his statement, whose final stanza returns to the central issue, with "dare" representing something like the *fait accompli*, in which he has participated. The mystery of the Tyger's creation has not been dispelled, but it has been looked at, it has provoked a recognition, and it has been incorporated by the speaker into a new sense of himself. At least some of his Selfhood has died to make way for new life, and he may now be able to deal with the deadly state of things he has dared to see.

The illustration in which the poem is set extends its verbal implications by various means. Several of the picture's elements are important in this regard. First, the Tyger is not fierce, but neither is like a cat essentially; rather, he is a cat with human features. Second, his stripes and those of the tree, the tree of Death, are almost indistinguishable, in some copies, especially where the two merge. And finally, it is the tree, somehow joined with or possibly sprung from the Tyger, that dominates the picture, though it seems to do so with less than maximum potential force. Obviously the Tyger first recognized by the speaker of the poem is very different from the Tyger depicted in the illustration. It seems reasonable to try to explain the difference between the two by assuming a development in meaning from the first to the second. Having written the poem, Blake provided for it a pictorial setting appropriate to its "ultimate" meaning. If the salient elements of the illustration are indeed a Tyger with crucially human features, a merger of human Tyger with the tree of Death and of the knowledge of good and evil, and the dominance of the world of the poem by that tree in a somewhat attenuated form of itself, then important correlations between text and picture are apparent.

First, the poem's tentative softening of the starkness of discrete and sometimes opposed entities is brought to partial resolution in the picture. In "The Lamb," speaker, child, Lamb, and Savior are identical: "I a child & thou a lamb, / We are called by his name." In "The Tyger," speaker, Tyger, Creator, and Lamb are in the first instance supposed to be very different. But the perceptual progress of the speaker, as it is indicated by his questions about the Tyger's Creator and the Lamb's, implies the inaccuracy of this initial view. The speaker of "The Tyger," who begins by seeing the Tyger as a unique terror, recognizes in the course of his thinking that he, with the rest of creation, is himself the Tyger in some sense. He who made the Lamb made the Tyger, and he made man as well, who is both Lamb and Tyger and more. In this perception of created things, it is appropriate that the human Tyger should not look terrifying; it is likewise appropriate that the tree of Death and of knowledge should be associated with the Tyger and with the speaker, who is responsible both for the creation of the Tyger and for the knowledge represented by the tree.

The discrete forces earlier perceived have not been so assimilated that the speaker has returned to Eden. (Lamb and Tyger do not lie down together.) Quite the contrary, what he has achieved is a new consciousness of his state, which includes his knowing that the world is overhung by the branches of the threatening tree associated with the loss of innocence and death. The illustration represents the fact that in the face of this recognition, the distance between himself and the Tyger who engendered the terrible vision in the first place is greatly closed. Both seem less than significant beneath that tree, though they give it life (the tree seems to grow out of them), and though the speaker has shown he has the visionary capacity to move beyond its inhibiting implications. Paradoxically increased and diminished by his experience, the speaker is for the moment in the condition of rest and hope. The deadly tree's leaflessness, the eagle of genius above, and the pink sky beyond are among the signs of his potential redemption. But his changing definition of himself is the chief sign, though it must for the moment appear to arrest hope entirely.

—Harold Pagliaro, *Selfhood and Redemption in Blake's Songs* (University Park: The Pennsylvania State University Press, 1987), 86–88.

[Martin K. Nurmi taught at Kent State University and co-authored *A Blake Bibliography* in 1977. He has also written numerous articles on and reviews of many of Blake's works. In this essay, "Blake's Revisions of 'The Tyger'", he explains how the changes reflect events transpiring in the world at the time of the poem's recomposition.]

It seems to me that the change of mood which we have observed Blake to pass through in his first two stages can be most easily accounted for as responses to events in France in the late summer and early autumn of 1792. Several lines of evidence converge to suggest this: the date of the drafts, the historical echoes in the pivotal fifth stanza and above all the fact that the course of the revolution in this period was, such that it could—and did—arouse this kind of response among humanitarian republicans.

Such cruel excesses of revolutionary energy as the Rising of the 10th of August and the September Massacres furnish a plausible occasion for Blake's troubled mood in the first stage. There was always something of the "gentle visionary" about Blake, and he must have deplored these early terrors, despite his ardent Jacobinism. Though his apocalypses may sometimes stream with blood (e.g., the end of *Milton*), he preferred to think of revolutions as bloodless, hoping in *The French Revolution* that the struggle would end by the king's soldier simply embracing the "meek peasant." Even in *America*, where he must treat a military victory won by American armies, he would rather not show the Americans as actually fighting; they merely "rush together," owing their victory to the fact of their solidarity and to the spiritual manifestation of revolution in the flaming Orc.

Then in late September came news that violence was apparently over, news which could have prompted the shift in mood seen in Blake's second stage. Viewed prophetically, such events as the defeat of the Austrians at Valmy on the 20th (to which Erdman, p. 178, has called attention in connection with the fifth stanza), the formation of the National Convention on the 21st, and the announcement of the French Republic on the 22nd must have made the attainment of Innocence seem close enough to cast the bloody actions of August and mid-September pretty well into the background. This view, according to Wordsworth and Coleridge, was even typical. The "lamentable crimes" of the September Massacres, writes Wordsworth, remembering the period after the announcement of the Republic,

> were past,
> Earth free from them for ever, as was thought,—
> Ephemeral monsters, to be seen but once!
> Things that could only show themselves and die.[1]

"The dissonance ceased," recalls Coleridge, "and all seemed calm and bright . . ."[2]

Blake is not, to be sure, writing merely a revolutionary lyric. His tiger is not another Orc, another portrayal of the spirit of revolt, but something much more inclusive, a symbol showing the creative power of energy, even of wrathful energy, wherever it appears. But because the revolution was for Blake a crucial contemporary manifestation of energy, events in the progress of the revolution would affect even his larger conception.[3]

For Blake to have been thus affected by contemporary events, his Notebook would have had to lie idle for a period of ten days or even several weeks, since the MS. drafts are on successive pages. This is easily possible. He did not write in his Notebook exclusively or constantly, but used it at this time for lyrics, which, according to H. M. Margoliouth, were written in response to events of one kind or another.[4] Moreover, if his uncertainty concerning such an important concept as that of energy was unresolved during his first stage, it is unlikely that he could work very productively until it was resolved, in the second stage. That an interruption did occur is suggested, indeed, by the appearance of the pages of the MS.—and even the appearance of a MS. page could conceivably have had some significance for the inventor of "illuminated printing." Whereas the first draft ends a page crowded with lyrics, the other drafts occupy a page that is otherwise blank, except for a light sketch. The empty space at the top of the second page, coming after the profusion of poems on the first, thus seems a visual parallel to the mournful and unproductive "blank in Nature" declared by Los in *Milton* (p. 383).

Blake's last revision is another matter. The final poem cannot be accounted for as a response to specific events. Though the Terror of late 1792 and early 1793 could have shown him that his relatively mild tiger of the second stage was premature, his restoration of dreadfulness to the poem in its final version does not show the influence of events—and certainly not of events like the Terror—as do his exaggerations of the two earlier stages. On the contrary, Blake's being able to handle dreadfulness and assimilate it in the unified symmetry of the final poem shows him to gain precisely that control of his material which his concern with revolution seems to have prevented him from gaining in his earlier stages. He is now able to transcend the limitations of specific events and give his symbol the comprehensive scope of an "eternal principle." This is the result of hard thought, not of events. Blake can now give the tiger's dreadfulness symbolic distance because he can see it in a perspective in which it no longer has the immediacy of an issue. And he can portray its symmetry as containing a really fearful component because he can see clearly and fully, at this point, the place of the tiger in the divine plan.

NOTES

1. Prelude (1850), ed. Ernest de Selincourt (London, 1926), x, 41–47.

2. "France: An Ode," *Poems*, ed. Ernest Hartley Coleridge (London, 1912), p. 245.

3. The Orc component of the tiger may be seen in the general similarities between the tiger and Orc in *America*, who, like the tiger, burns in the night as if he had been forged, glowing "as the wedge / Of iron heated in the furnace" (p. 202), and whose origin is a little ambiguously either in the Satanic deeps or the divine Atlantic mountains (p. 202). Very bloody revolutionary tigers indeed are associated with Orc in Europe, where Enitharmon's premature belief that Eden had come—a situation parallel to Blake's 2nd stage of composition—is shattered by the resumption of strife (p. 219). These tigers, however, are far removed from the tiger of the poem, representing a limit of this use of the symbol by Blake. Blake's later disillusionment with Orc in 1801 (as Napoleon—Erdman, p. 292) is parallel to his use of the "forms of tygers & of Lions" to show men "dishumanized" by war in night vi of *The Four Zoas* (p. 303). (The edition of Blake cited is *Blake's Poetry and Prose*, ed. Geoffrey Keynes (London, 1948).—Ed.]

4. *William Blake* (London, 1951), p. 54. Margoliouth remarks that the occasion of *The Tyger* is unknown, but believes that this poem is occasional (p. 58).

—Martin K. Nurmi, "Blake's Revisions of 'The Tyger,'" *Twentieth-Century Interpretations of Songs* of Innocence and of Experience, ed. Morton D. Paley (Englewood Cliffs: Prentice Hall, 1969), 104–106.

STEWART CREHAN ON "THE TYGER" AS A SIGN OF REVOLUTIONARY TIMES

[Stewart Crehan is a Professor of English at the University of the Transkei in South Africa. He has written *Blake in Context* and *Nature's Excess: Physiocratic Theory and Romanticism*. In *Blake in Context*, Crehan shows how the work is informed by the historical, political, and social changes of the era.]

The Tyger is a response to the terrible, new-born beauty of violent revolution. The poet now confronts his own antinomian energies as an external creation, whose 'fearful symmetry' obeys no known laws, and yet has a manifest, organised (and ferocious) presence. Whether as subjective potentiality or as political upheaval, the Tyger cannot be ignored:

> Tyger! Tyger! burning bright
> In the forests of the night,
> What immortal hand or eye
> Could frame thy fearful symmetry?

Blake conveys violent, revolutionary energy by his use of a resonating poetic symbol (the wild beast in the forest) and the invention of a *persona*, whose thirteen unanswered questions, bound by the six hammered stanzas, give the poem its peculiarly compressed verbal power.

Blake's dual symbol had a history. More important, it had a political context. By examining both, the contextual meaning of the poem becomes clearer.

In the opening of Dante's *Inferno*, the poet is seen trying to leave the dark wood of Error, which is 'savage and harsh and dense', but he is turned back by wild animals—the leopard of incontinence, the lion of bestiality and the wolf of malice and fraud. Wild beasts symbolise the dehumanisation of man through sin: whereas unfallen man is noble and godlike, sinful man is bestial; wild beasts are the sign of his degradation. In Milton's *Comus*, the dark wood reappears as a 'close dungeon of unnumerable boughs', where Comus the enchanter and his 'rout of monsters' make their 'riotous and unruly noise'. Each has been changed

> Into some brutish form of wolf, or bear,
> Or ounce, or tiger, hog or bearded goat

—or, again, they prowl in the hideous wood 'Like stabled wolves, or tigers at their prey'. Placed in its social and political context, and mediated through Milton's puritan consciousness, this monstrous rout of bestial passions can be equated with the licentious rapacity of a depraved aristocracy; on the other hand, it might just as easily be the brutalised and intemperate mob. Comus' unruly train have the qualities of both.

Wild passions in dark woods inevitably carry social as well as psychological implications. The dark recesses of the soul can often be traced to their social locations. Bearing in mind, then, the traditional meanings of the dual symbol (fallen man, bestial passion, social depravity), what immediately strikes us about Blake's poem is not—as Kathleen Raine would have it—that the Tyger is 'a symbol of competitive, predatious selfhood', but that this 'predatious selfhood' has acquired a new splendour. Moreover, the beast in question had leapt to the centre of consciousness in such a way that the speaker is unable to judge it or categorise it according to traditional schemas; the emblem has burst out of its religious frame. There is even the feeling that this old symbol of bestial passion may be the one point of purifying, if destructive brightness in the traditional forests of Error.

In an important essay, Martin K. Nurmi argued that Blake's *The Tyger* was a direct response to events in France, and that the 'cruel excesses' of the August Rising and the September Massacres of 1792 provoked an initially horrified reaction (hence the 'horrid ribs' and 'sanguine woe' in the first draft), but that this was modified when the National Convention was formed (21 September) and the French Republic was announced (22 September). The final draft, says Nurmi, was 'the result of hard thought, not of events'; the tiger's 'dreadfulness' could now be seen in perspective, as part of 'the divine plan'. This is convincing, but it is not the only evidence for the poem's topicality. *The Tyger* is a symbolist poem. By unearthing the currency of Blake's symbol at the time he wrote the poem, we might gain a further insight into its political meaning.

It can be argued, in fact, that Blake was not only consciously transforming a traditional symbolism, but that he was criticising, through the speaker of *The Tyger*, a prevailing conservative ideology that viewed revolution merely as a horrifying, dehumanising process.

—Stewart Crehan, *Blake in Context* (Dublin: Gill and Macmillan Humanities Press, 1984), 125–127.

Morton D. Paley on Differing Viewpoints on "The Tyger"

[Morton D. Paley is a Professor Emeritus of English at the University of California at Berkeley and edits *Blake: An Illustrated Quarterly*. He is the author of a study on Blake's thought called *Energy and the Imagination*. In this essay, "Tyger of Wrath", Paley compares and contrasts scholars' varying points of view on the poem.]

Swinburne reads the poem as a piece of Romantic Satanism. Making use of Blake's Notebook, then in the possession of Dante Gabriel Rossetti, Swinburne prints an earlier version of the second stanza, then paraphrases it and some of the rest of the poem as follows:

> Burnt in distant deeps or skies
> The cruel fire of thine eyes?
> Could heart descend or wings aspire?
> What the hand dare seize the fire?

Could God bring down his heart to the making of a thing so deadly and strong? or could any lesser daemonic force of nature take to itself wings and fly high enough to assume power equal to such a creation? Could spiritual force so far descend or material force so far aspire? Or, when the very stars, and all the armed children of heaven, the "helmed cherubim" that guide and the "sworded seraphim" that guard their several planets, wept for pity and fear at sight of this new force of monstrous matter seen in the deepest night as a fire of menace to man—

Did he smile his work to see?
Did he who made the lamb make thee?[10]

By calling the Tyger a "new force of monstrous matter" and "a fire of menace to man," Swinburne distorts the question. He also ignores the typical meaning of stars in Blake's symbolism as well as the significance of a cancelled stanza's being a cancelled stanza. Yeats and Ellis, editors of the first collection of Blake's complete works, take a different view in their brief comment: "The 'Tiger' is, of course, the tiger of wrath, wiser in his own way than the horse of instruction, but always, like the roaring of lions and the destructive sword, so terrible as to be a portion of eternity too great for the eye of man.'"[11] S. Foster Damon, in his monumental *William Blake: His Philosophy and Symbols*, first published in 1924, finds the question of the poem to be "how to reconcile the Forgiveness of Sins (the Lamb) with the Punishment of Sins (the Tyger)." The Wrath of the Tyger had to be of divine origin ("His God was essentially personal; therefore Evil must be his Wrath"). The purpose of Wrath is "to consume Error, to annihilate those stubborn beliefs which cannot be removed by the tame 'horses of instruction.'" Yet Damon also thinks that "Did he who made the Lamb make thee?" is "not an exclamation of wonder, but a very real question, whose answer Blake was not sure of."[12]

For Joseph H. Wicksteed, author of the most detailed commentary on the *Songs*, the poem's questions do seem to have a definite answer. "The whole thesis of 'The Tyger,'" he writes, "is that he is a spiritual expression of the Creator himself . . . 'The Tyger' is a tremendous treatise enunciating the nature of the God that *does* exist—the God that is mightily and terribly visible in his manifestations." Attempting to discover the history of Blake's inner life through the visions and revisions of the Notebook, Wicksteed decided that "the composition of this great poem registers (perhaps effects) a change in Blake's mind," carrying him beyond the world view of the *Songs of Experience* to that of the prophecies.[13]

Since the time of these pioneer critics, writers on the poem have continued to disagree about whether the Tyger is "good," created by the Lamb's creator; ambiguous, its creator unknown and the question of the poem unanswerable; or "evil," created by some maleficent force. The first of these views has been given succinct expression by Mark Schorer:

> The juxtaposition of lamb and tiger points not merely to the opposition of innocence and experience, but to the resolution of the paradox they present. The innocent impulses of the lamb have been curbed by restraints, and the lamb has turned into something else, indeed into the tiger. Innocence is converted to experience. It does not rest there. Energy can be curbed but it cannot be destroyed, and when it reaches the limits of its endurance, it bursts forth in revolutionary wrath.[14]

Similar to Schorer's interpretation in this respect are those of David V. Erdman, Stanley Gardner, Martin K. Nurmi, F. W. Bateson, and Martin Price.[15]

Among those who have seen the Tyger as either ambiguous or ambivalent are Northrop Frye, Hazard Adams, Robert F. Gleckner, John E. Grant, Paul Miner, E. D. Hirsch, Jr., and Philip Hobsbaum. Frye advises the reader of the poem to "leave it a question." Adams, in his generally valuable essay on "The Tyger," finds two views within the poem; however, he emphasizes the "visionary" one, according to which "the tiger symbolizes the primal spiritual energy which may bring form out of chaos and unite man with that part of his own being which he has allowed somehow to sleep walk into the dreadful forests of material darkness." Gleckner, setting "The Tyger" against some passages in *The Four Zoas*, also finds two views. Grant, in his finely considered discussion, "The Art and Argument of 'The Tyger,'" indicates agreement with Wicksteed but, unlike Wicksteed, finds only conditional answers.

> If he who made the Lamb also made the Tyger, it is because the two beasts are contraries . . . . If the creator smiles because he sees that in the end the Tyger will leave the forest along with man, a man may feel justified in asking why it is his lot now to be cast among savage beasts. This question cannot be removed from "The Tyger," and, in spite of assertions to the contrary, it was one of the questions which continued to concern Blake throughout his life.

Both Miner and Hirsch find two different perspectives maintained throughout the poem, though they see its final answer as affirmative. Hobsbaum cautions readers against answering the questions, as he regards Blake himself as being in doubt about them.[16]

Two recent commentators on the poem consider the Tyger to be perceived as evil. Harold Bloom regards this perception as the error of the "speaker" of the poem, which he thinks of as a monologue delivered by a Bard in the fallen state of Experience. "The Bard of Experience is in mental darkness . . . The Bard is one of the Redeemed, capable of imaginative salvation, but before the poem ends he has worked his frenzy into the self-enclosure of the Elect Angels, prostrate before a mystery entirely of his own creation."[17] This Bard, whom I cannot help regarding as entirely read into the poem, would resemble Adams' shadowy first speaker, for whom the creator of the Tyger must be a Urizenic God, a "devil-maker."[18] Miss Kathleen Raine, pursuing a different method, comes to a parallel conclusion: that the creator of the Tyger is such a devil-maker. She suggests sources in Gnostic and Hermetic mysticism as proof that "the Lamb was made by the son of God, the second person of the Trinity . . . the Tiger was made by the demiurge, the third person of the (Gnostic and Cabbalistic) trinity. Lamb and Tiger inhabit different worlds, and are the work of different creators." To Miss Raine the Tyger seems "a symbol of competitive, predacious selfhood."[19]

The meaning of "The Tyger" has been and continues to be disputed. I would like to suggest that our understanding of the poem can be deepened and enhanced if we regard it against the traditions I have mentioned: that of Jakob Boehme, his predecessor Paracelsus, and his disciple William Law; and that of the British theoreticians of the sublime in the eighteenth century. These disparate traditions have at least one nexus other than their meeting in the mind of William Blake: for quite different reasons, the expression of the Wrath of God in the Bible, particularly in the Old Testament, is of great importance to each of them. This Biblical material also bears directly on Blake's theme in "The Tyger." I shall propose that "The Tyger" is an apostrophe to Wrath as a "sublime" phenomenon, to Wrath both in the Prophetic sense and as what Boehme calls the First Principle. The images and rhetoric of the poem will be found to support such an interpretation.

NOTES

10. London, 1868, p. 120. For Blake's actual spelling and punctuation, see *The Complete Writings of William Blake*, ed. Geoffrey Keynes (London, 1966), pp. 172, 173, 214. This edition will hereafter be cited as K.

11. Edwin John Ellis and William Butler Yeats, *The Works of William Blake* (London, 1893), II, 14.

12. Pp. 277–278.

13. *Blake's Innocence and Experience* (London, 1928), pp. 196, 212.

14. *William Blake: The Politics of Vision* (New York, 1946), pp. 250–251.

15. Erdman, *Blake: Prophet Against Empire* (Princeton, 1954), pp. 179–180. Erdman, like Schorer, regards the questions of the poem as rhetorical. Gardner, *Infinity on the Anvil* (Oxford, 1954), pp. 123–130. Nurmi, "Blake's Revisions of *The Tyger*," *PMLA*, LXXI (1956), 669–685. [An excerpt from this essay is included among the selections in this volume.] Bateson, *Selected Poems of William Blake*, pp. 117–119. Price, *To the Palace of Wisdom* (Garden City, N.Y.), 1964, pp. 398–400. [See "The Vision of Innocence," included among the selections in this volume.]

16. Frye, "Blake After Two Centuries," *UTQ*, XXVII (1957), 12. Adams, *William Blake: A Reading of the Shorter Poems* (Seattle, 1963), p. 73. Gleckner, *The Piper & the Bard* (Detroit, 1959), pp. 275–290. [An extract from this book is included among the selections in this volume.] Grant (ed.), *Discussions of William Blake* (Boston, 1961), p. 75. Miner, "'The Tyger': Genesis and Evolution in the Poetry of William Blake," *Criticism*, IV (1962), 59–73. Hirsch, *Innocence and Experience: An Introduction to Blake* (New Haven, 1964), pp. 244–252. Hobsbaum, "A Rhetorical Question Answered: Blake's Tyger and Its Critics," *Neophilologus*, XLVIII (1964), 151–155.

17. *Blake's Apocalypse* (Garden City, N.Y., 1963), pp. 137–138.

18. *William Blake*, p. 65.

19. "Who Made the Tyger?" *Encounter*, II (1954). 48, 43

　　　—Morton D. Paley, "Tyger of Wrath." In *Twentieth-Century Interpretations of Songs* of Innocence and of Experience, ed. Morton D. Paley (Englewood Cliffs: Prentice Hall, 1969), 70–74.

MARTIN PRICE ON TERROR AND SYMMETRY IN "THE TYGER"

[Martin Price of Yale University wrote *To the Palace of Wisdom* and *Swift's Rhetorical Art*. In the essay, "The Vision of Innocence", he offers another interpretation of this work, considering complex imagery and confusion in "The Tyger".]

'The Tyger' is the best known of Blake's songs and the most frequently and elaborately interpreted. The phrase 'fearful symmetry'—whatever its possible symbolic suggestions—is clearly the initial puzzle: the 'symmetry' implies an ordering hand or intelligence, the 'fearful' throws doubt on the benevolence of the Creator. The 'forests of the night' are the darkness out of which the tiger looms, brilliant in contrast; they, also embody the doubt or confusion that surrounds the origins of the tiger. In the case of 'The Lamb', the Creator 'calls himself a Lamb. / He is meek, & he is mild; / He became a little child'. In 'The Tyger' the Creator again is like what he creates, and the form that must be supplied him now is the Promethean smith working violently at his forge. The last alteration we have of this much altered poem insists upon the likeness of Creator and created: 'What dread hand Form'd thy dread feet?' The tiger is an image of the Creator; its 'deadly terrors' must be His.

The most puzzling stanza of the poem is the next-to-last:

> When the stars threw down their spears,
> And water'd heaven with their tears,
> Did he smile his work to see?
> Did he who made the Lamb make-thee?

The first two lines are the crux of the poem. (. . .)

The 'spiritual sword / That lays open the hidden heart' is a counterpart of the tiger we see in the *Songs of Experience*. The wrath serves the ultimate end of redemption and becomes one with mercy. If the God of apparent wrath is also the God of forgiveness, the tiger's form is only superficially 'fearful'. In the words of Pope:

> Nor God alone in the still calm we find,
> He mounts the storm, and walks upon the wind
> (*Essay on Man*, II, 109–10).

'The Tyger' dramatizes the terrors of the shocked doubter, but it moves with assurance—in the stanza I have quoted—to an assertion of faith (faith in the oneness of God, in the goodness of wrath, in the holiness of prophetic rage). When the last stanza repeats the first, but for the alteration of 'could' to 'dare,' the question has been answered. The inconceivable of the first stanza has become the majestic certainty of the last: the daring of the Creator—whether God or man—is the cleansing wrath of the tiger.

—Martin Price, "The Vision of Innocence," *Critics on Blake: Readings in Literary Criticism*, ed. Judith O'Neill (Coral Gables: University of Miami Press, 1970), 106–107.

"London"

It is impossible to study William Blake's "London" without an understanding of the time in which it was written; in Blake's opinion, the Industrial Revolution had changed the city for worse. The manufacturing work being done in factories created filth and pollution. London was dirty. Thick, black smoke from factories left behind a nasty residue where it landed. The river Thames was polluted with the byproducts of industry. The new type of work changed the city socially, economically, and topographically. Although the new industrial economy created many jobs, the wages of these jobs were low. Long hours of hard labor did not guarantee a living wage. The poor worked themselves to death in unsafe, unsanitary, and unhealthful conditions. The suffering in the streets of the city affected Blake profoundly. While he could not change society, he could observe, and express his opinion of the changes in his art.

Scholars point to the many versions of this poem found in Blake's notes. Writing and re-writing, Blake edited his work down to every detail. Carefully selected words paint a bleak picture of London life in the late 18th century. Looking at the language he chose in previous drafts of the poem, students of Blake find he was very deliberate in his selections. His word choices are important on many levels. Scholars devote chapters to the selection of one word in the finished version of one work. Blake considered the impact of each vivid description before "London" was finished. Understanding the multiple meanings of words and being familiar with history are some of the background needed to fully grasp and appreciate the poem. An early draft began the poem:

> I wander thro each dirty street
> Near where the dirty Thames does flow

whereas the finished version reads:

> I wander thro' each charter'd street
> Near where the charter'd Thames does flow

The change from *dirty* to *charter'd* is significant. *Charter'd* is a word of multiple meanings. According to E.P. Thompson, *charter'd* is associated with commerce and cheating. A *charter* is also a document that grants rights to individuals, at the same time limiting the rights of others. The semantic instability of such choices forms the basis of much of the body of Blake criticism.

The speaker starts by searching the streets of London for inspiration, planning to describe what he sees there. What he finds is troubling: "weakness" and "woe" in the face of every person he meets. It's a weary life for people in Blake's London.

In the second verse, we find more despair; it becomes a common thread in the fabric of London life. Every man, every woman, and every child can expect life and the law to produce the same misery. The challenges of life in London weigh heavy on the minds of citizens. Blake believes Londoners are shackled to an unpleasant life and that the worst of it is that the Londoners' imprisonment is of their own conception. How can one break free when thought has created the prison? Where can a Londoner find relief? Is there any peace for weary workers or comfort for a wounded spirit? Not in these four verses.

The third verse vividly shows us what Blake means. It provides an extremely grim picture of life in London, a worst-case scenario. Chimney sweeps faced some of the worst working conditions of the day. They worked outdoors at great heights, affected by the elements, the ubiquitous smog of London, and their own fear. The work was exhausting. They inhaled the layers of soot and ash that they cleaned from the chimneys, and what they didn't inhale ended up on their clothing. Furthermore, the job was seasonal, and many were left to beg for a living when their brooms were not busy. This was a sad image of a working life: when on the job, he risked life and limb to provide for his family, and when not working he faced desperation in the streets. The chimney sweep was forced to ask for charity. By Blake's standards, the job that cost so much personally offered little in the way of satisfaction.

Nor is the House of God a source of comfort for the speaker of "London": the image of the "Blackening Church" is particularly troubling. The environment of London is causing physical and spiritual decay. Industrialization is polluting the outer structure of the churches. Inside, those seeking salvation have trouble finding it. The hard work in the factories and the bleak outlook on life is "blackening" the hearts the faithful. Instead of enlightenment, religion has become just another obligation. Instead of strengthening spirits, the churches impede peace. Blake's opinions on organized religion, particularly on Swedenborgism, or the Church of the New Jerusalem, appear in other poems, satirically, as well.

According to the speaker, Londoners are finding no comfort in prayer and no solace in the monarchy. Behind the palace walls, England's reigning family is removed from the strife in the streets. The King fails to address the problems facing the working people. Soldiers, sighing, blood: the images are bleak. England is losing its people to the Industrial Revolution and to the American Revolution. There is blood on the palace walls because of the losing battles: gone are both a part of the Empire and a way of life.

As Blake brings "London" to a close, we find that night, too, is powerless to bring peace to the crowded streets of the city, that darkness does not disguise despair. The speaker describes what he hears: Prostitutes curse. Babies cry. And why shouldn't they cry? The life into which they have been born is not an easy one. It is not comfortable and promises no joy. Parents find married life unsatisfying. Blake frames the union of woman and man in terms of crisis and death, and the last word of the poem is *hearse*. Indeed, this may be the only place in which a citizen in Blake's "London" can find rest. The hard life is finally over: a beaten spirit can leave the misery of the streets.

Family life in "London" is difficult, work is hard, the streets are dirty, and the air is filthy. There is little comfort in religion or in patriarchy. For Blake's speaker, the late 18th century is a terrible time in which to be living in London.

"London"

DAVID V. ERDMAN ON PEOPLE IN BLAKE'S "LONDON"

[David V. Erdman taught at the State University of New York at Stony Brook. He edited *The Poetry and Prose of William Blake* and wrote *Blake: Prophet Against Empire* and *Concordance of the Works of Blake*. He also was editor of publications at the New York Public Library. In this writing, Erdman explores the ways in which the lives of 18th-century London influenced Blake's vision of the city.]

When we turn now to 'London', Blake's 'mightiest brief poem',[10] our minds ringing with Blakean themes, we come upon infinite curses in a little room, a world at war in a grain of London soot. On the illuminated page a child is leading a bent old man along the cobblestones and a little vagabond is warming his hands at a fire in the open street. But it is Blake who speaks . . . .

In his first draft Blake wrote 'dirty street' and 'dirty Thames' as plain statement of fact, reversing the sarcastic 'golden London' and 'silver Thames' of his early parody of Thomson's 'Rule Britannia'. And the harlot's curse sounded in every 'dismal' street. The change to 'charter'd' (with an intermediate 'cheating')[11] mocks Thomson's boast that 'the charter of the land' keeps Britons free, and it suggests agreement with (perhaps was even suggested by) Paine's condemnation of 'charters and corporations' in the Second Part of *The Rights of Man*, where Paine argues that all charters are purely negative in effect and that city charters, by annulling the rights of the majority, cheat the inhabitants and destroy the town's prosperity— even London being 'capable of bearing up against the political evils of a corporation' only from its advantageous situation on the Thames.[12] Paine's work was circulated by shopkeepers chafing under corporation rule and weary, like Blake, of the 'cheating waves of charter'd streams' of monopolized commerce (*N*. 113).

In the notebook fragment just quoted Blake speaks of shrinking 'at the little blasts of fear That the hireling blows into my ear', thus indicating that when he writes of the 'mind-forg'd manacles' in every cry of fear and every ban he is not saying simply that people are voluntarily forging manacles in their own minds. Hireling informers or mercenaries promote the fear; Pitt's proclamations are the bans, linked with an order to dragoons 'to assemble on Hounslow Heath' and 'be within one hour's march of the metropolis'.[13] A rejected reading, 'german forged links', points to several manacles forged ostensibly in the mind of Hanoverian George: the Prussian manoeuvres on the heath, the British alliance with Prussia and Austria against France, and the landing of Hessian and Hanoverian mercenaries in England allegedly en route to battlefronts in France.

Blake may have written 'London' before this last development, but before he completed his publication there was a flurry of alarm among freeborn Englishmen at the presence of German hirelings. 'Will you wait till BARRACKS are erected in every village,' exclaimed a London Corresponding Society speaker in January 1794, 'and till subsidized Hessians and Hanoverians are upon us?"[14] In Parliament Lord Stanhope expressed the hope that honest Britons would meet this Prussian invasion 'by OPPOSING FORCE BY FORCE'. And the editor of *Politics for the People*, reporting that one Hessian had stabbed an Englishman in a street quarrel, cried that all were brought 'to cut the throats of Englishmen'. He urged citizens to arm and to fraternize with their fellow countrymen, the British common soldiers.[15]

The latter are Blake's 'hapless Soldiers' whose 'sigh Runs in blood down Palace walls'—and whose frequently exhibited inclination in 1792–1793 to turn from grumbling to mutiny[16] is not taken into account by those who interpret the blood as the soldier's own and who overlook the potentially forceful meaning of 'sigh' in eighteenth century diction.[17] In the structure of the poem the soldier's utterance that puts blood on palace walls is parallel to the harlot's curse that blasts and blights. And Blake would have known that curses were often chalked or painted on the royal walls. In October 1792 Lady Malmesbury's Louisa saw 'written upon the Privy Garden-wall, "No coach-tax; d—Pitt! d—n the Duke of Richmond! *no King*"'.[18]

A number of cognate passages in which Blake mentions blood on palace walls indicate that the blood is an apocalyptic omen of mutiny and civil war involving regicide. In *The French Revolution* people and soldiers fraternize, and when their 'murmur' (sigh) reaches the palace, blood runs down the ancient pillars. In *The Four Zoas*, Night I, similar 'wailing' affects the people; 'But most the polish'd Palaces, dark, silent, bow with dread.' 'But most' is a phrase straight from 'London'. And in Night IX the people's sighs and cries of fear mount to 'furious' rage, apocalyptic blood 'pours down incessant', and 'Kings in their palaces lie drownd' in it, torn 'limb from limb'.[19] In the same passage the marks of weakness and woe of 'London' are spelled out as 'all the marks . . . of the slave's scourge & tyrant's crown'. In 'London' Blake is talking about what he hears in the streets, about the moral stain of the battlefield sigh of expiring soldiers.

NOTES

10. Oliver Elton's phrase, I forgot where.

11. The 'cheating' variant is in *N.* 113; see E464, 772/K166.

12. Paine, I, 407; Nancy Bogen (*Notes and Queries*, XV, January 1968) finds Paine also calling 'every chartered town . . . an aristocratic monopoly' in the First Part (1791) as well. On chartered boroughs see Cowper, *The Task*, iv. 671; also John Butler, *Brief Reflections*, 1791, a pamphlet reply to Burke cited in J. T. Boulton, *The Language of Politics in the Age of Wilkes and Burke*, Toronto, 1963, p. 193.

13. *Gazette*, Dec. 1, 1792. In the note just cited, Mrs Bogen suggests that Blake's choice, in the Thames poem, of the Ohio as the river to wash Thames stains from a Londoner 'born a slave' and aspiring 'to be free' was influenced by Gilbert Imlay's *Topographical Description*, London, 1792. On the Ohio Imlay found escape from 'musty forms' that 'lead you into labyrinths of doubt and perplexity' and freedom from priestcraft which elsewhere 'seems to have forged fetters for the human mind'.

14. Address at Globe Tavern, Jan. 20, 1794 (pamphlet).

15. Eaton, *Politics for the People*, II, no. 7, March 15, 1794.

16. The Royal Proclamation cited efforts to 'delude the judgment of the lower classes' and 'debauch the soldiery. Wilberforce feared that 'the soldiers are everywhere tampered with. Gilbert Elliot in November expressed a common belief that armies and navies would prove 'but brittle weapons' against the spreading French ideas. *Life and Letters of Sir Gilbert Elliot First Earl of Minto*,

3 vols., London, 1874, ɪɪ, 74. Through the winter and spring there were sporadic attacks of the populace on press gangs and recruiting houses. Mutiny and rumours of mutiny were reported in the *General Evening Post*, Apr. 20, July 20, Aug. 3, 7, 31, Oct. 28, 30, 1793. In Ireland the mutiny of embodied regiments broached into a small civil war. See also Lucyle Werkmeister, *A Newspaper History of England*, 1792–1793, Lincoln, Neb., 1968, items indexed under 'Insurrection, phantom', and 'Ireland'.

17. S. Foster Damon, *William Blake: His Philosophy and Symbols*, Boston and London, 1924, p. 283, reads it as the battlefield 'death-sigh' which morally 'is a stain upon the State'. Joseph H. Wicksteed, *Blake's Innocence & Experience*, N.Y., 1928, p. 253, has it that the soldier who promotes peace is quelling the 'tumult and war' of a 'radically unstable' society. But Blake was not one to look upon riot-quelling as a securing of freedom and peace! Alfred Kazin, *The Portable Blake*, p. 15, with a suggestion 'that the Soldier's desperation runs, like his own blood, in accusation down the walls of the ruling Palace', comes closer to the spirit of indignation which Blake reflects.

18. Elliot, ɪɪ, 71. Verbally Blake's epithet may be traced back, I suppose, to 'hapless Warren!', Barlow's phrase for the patriot general dying at Bunker Hill (changed to 'glorious Warren' in 1793).

19. *F.R.* 241–246: K145; *F.Z.* i. 396: K275; ix. 73–74, 230–255: K359,363.

> —David V. Erdman, "Infinite London: The *Songs of Experience* in their Historical Setting," *Critics on Blake: Readings in Literary Criticism*, ed. Judith O'Neill (Coral Gables: University of Miami Press, 1970), 65–68.

Kenneth Johnston on the Vocabulary of Blake's "London"

[Kenneth Johnston is a Professor of English at Indiana University. He has written *The Hidden Wordsworth: Poet, Lover, Rebel, Spy* and edited *Romantic Revolutions: Theory and Criticism* and *The Age of William Wordsworth*. This essay, like Erdman's above, examines the people of London. Johnson believes Blake sees the people of the city victims of circumstance. He explains how the artwork and the words combine to paint a harsh picture of daily life.]

The chimney sweeper, the conscripted soldier, and the prostitute in the poem are undeniably victims, but Blake's changes point to his conviction that repression is not simply the result of "bans" handed down from above. German George III issues the bans, Blake knows, but even he cannot forge the manacles with which we shackle our spirits into obeying them; man's "marks of weakness" are partially the cause of his "marks of woe."

The design across the top of *London* {18} is an excellent example of the way in which Blake's designs at their best enrich the verbal statement of the poems. Because it does not relate directly to anything in the text, the design at first confuses, but its effect does jar the reader's perceptions out of the verbal and into the visual mode. On first viewing, the aged cripple and the child who seems to be leading him appear as two victims of the evils of contemporary London, but on closer inspection—of independent visual elements counterpointing independent verbal elements—we recognize a dramatization of the statement of the first stanza: the child and the ancient "mark" (see) in each other's face "woe" and "weakness," respectively. Or, more simply (since the old man may be blind), they *are* the marks—evidences—themselves. Furthermore, there is a profound irony in the situation if, as seems likely, the child is supposed to be leading the old man. Viewed against the text this is a mockery, since every stanza after the first contains a detail about the victimization of children in London. But what seems a mockery to common sense may be a profoundly sustained ironic contrast to the author of *The Marriage of Heaven and Hell*. If we generalize the child as Innocence and the aged cripple as Experience, we can interpret the design in the larger context of the *Songs Of Innocence and Of Experience, Shewing the Two Contrary States of the Human Soul*. Does the design parallel the text by showing the inadequacies of Innocence and Experience as *separated* modes of consciousness, or is it to be read counter to the text, as a hopeful sign of human progress, a glimpse of the day when the wisdom of Experience moves forward in the city guided by the fresh simplicity of Innocent desires?[7]

NOTE

7. Cf. John Grant, "The Colors of Prophecy," *The Nation*, CC (25 January 1965), 92; E. D. Hirsch, *Innocence and Experience: An Introduction to Blake*, New Haven, 1964, 265. Both Grant and Hirsch see the design optimistically contrary to the text. Hirsch sees both the old man and the child as emblems of weakness and woe: "Like the poem, the design telescopes cause and effect."

—Kenneth Johnston, "Blake's Cities: Romantic Forms of Urban Renewal," *Blake's Visionary Forms Dramatic*, ed. David V. Erdman and John E. Grant (Princeton: Princeton University Press, 1970), 417–419.

E.P. THOMPSON ON THE WAYS IN WHICH WORDS CHANGE "LONDON"

[E.P. Thompson authored *Witness Against the Beast: William Blake and the Moral Law*. In this essay, Thompson takes a look at Blake's revisions in the writing of "London". He shows us how some seemingly simple changes have a major impact on the images and meaning of the work.]

Thus 'charter'd' arose in Blake's mind in association with 'cheating' and with the 'little blasts of fear' of the 'hireling'. The second association is an obvious political allusion. To reformers the corrupt political system was a refuge for hirelings: indeed, Dr. Johnson had defined in his dictionary a 'Pension' as 'in England it is generally understood to mean pay given to a state hireling for treason to his country.' David Erdman is undoubtedly right that the 'little blasts of fear' suggest the proclamations, the Paine-burnings, and the political repressions of the State and of Reeves's Association for Preserving Liberty and Property against Republicans and Levellers which dominated the year in which these poems were written.[4] In the revised version of 'Thames' Blake introduces the paradox which was continually to be in the mouths of radicals and factory reformers in the next fifty years: the slavery of the English poor. And he points also ('I was born a slave but I go to be free') to the first wave of emigration of reformers from the attention of Church-and-King mobs or hirelings.

But 'charter'd' is more particularly associated with 'cheating.' It is clearly a word to be associated with commerce: one might think of the Chartered Companies which, increasingly drained of function, were bastions of privilege within the government of the city. Or, again, one might think of the monopolistic privileges of the East India Company, whose ships were so prominent in the commerce of the Thames, which applied in 1793 for twenty years' renewal of its charter, and which was under bitter attack in the reformers' press.[5]

But 'charter'd' is, for Blake, a stronger and more complex word than that, which he endows with more generalized symbolic power. It has the feel of a word which Blake has recently discovered, as, years later, he was to 'discover' the word 'golden' (which, nevertheless, he had been using for years). He is savouring it, weighing its poetic possibilities in his hand. It is in no sense a 'new' word, but he has found a way to use it with a new ironic inversion. For the word is standing at an intellectual and political cross-roads. On the one hand it was a stale counter of the customary libertarian rhetoric of the polite culture. Blake himself had used it in much this way in his early 'King Edward the Third':

> Let Liberty, the charter'd right of Englishmen,
> Won by our fathers in many a glorious field,
> Enerve my soldiers; let Liberty
> Blaze in each countenance, and fire the battle.
> The enemy fight in chains, invisible chains, but heavy;
> Their minds are fetter'd; then how can they be free?[6]

It would be only boring to accumulate endless examples from eighteenth-century constitutional rhetoric or poetry of the use of chartered rights, chartered liberties, magna carta: the word is at the centre of Whig ideology.

There is, however, an obvious point to be made about this tedious usage of 'charter'. A charter of liberty is, simultaneously, a denial of these liberties to others. A charter is something given or ceded; it is bestowed upon some group by some authority; it is not claimed as of right. And the liberties (or privileges) granted to this guild, company, corporation or even nation *exclude* others from the enjoyment of these liberties. A charter is, in its nature, exclusive.

NOTES

4. See David Erdman, *Blake: Prophet against Empire*, revised edn. (New York, 1969) which fully argues these points on pp. 272–9. These poems were 'forged in the heat of the Year One of Equality (September 1792 to 1793) and tempered in the "grey-brow'd snows" of Antijacobin alarms and proclamations'. See also A. Mitchell. 'The Association Movement of 1792–3', *Historical Journal*, IV: 1 (1961), 56–77; E. P. Thompson, *The Making of the English Working Class* (Harmondsworth, 1968), pp. 115–26; D. E. Ginter, 'The Loyalist Association Movement, 1792–3', *Historical Journal*, IV: 2 (1966), 179–90.

5. 'The cheating waves of charter'd streams' and 'the cheating banks of Thames' should prompt one to think carefully of this as the source which first gave to Blake this use of 'charter'd'. The fullest attack from a Painite source on the East India Company did not appear until 1794: see the editorial articles in four successive numbers of Daniel Isaac Eaton's *Politics for the People*, II: 8–11 : 'The East India Charter Considered'. These constituted a full-blooded attack on the Company's commercial and military imperialism ('If it be deemed expedient to *murder* half the inhabitants of India, and *rob* the remainder, surely it is not requisite to call it *governing* them?') which carried to their furthest point criticisms of the Company to be found in the reforming and Foxite press of 1792–3. No social historian can be surprised to find the banks of the Thames described as 'cheating' in the eighteenth century: every kind of fraud and racket, big, small and indifferent, flourished around the docks. The association of the banks of Thames with commerce was already traditional when Samuel Johnson renewed it in his 'London' (1738), esp. lines 20–30. Johnson's attitude is already ambiguous: 'Britannia's glories' ('The guard of commerce, and the dread of Spain') are invoked retrospectively, in conventional terms: but on Thames-side already 'all are slaves to gold, / Where looks are merchandise, and smiles are sold'. Erdman argues that the 'golden London' and 'silver Thames' of Blake's 'King Edward the Third' have already assimilated this conventional contrast in the form of irony: see Erdman, *Prophet against Empire*, pp. 80–1.

6. E415/K18: If we take the intention of this fragment to be ironic, then Blake was already regarding the word as suspect rhetoric.

—E.P. Thompson, "London." In *Interpreting Blake*, ed. M. Phillips (Cambridge: Cambridge University Press, 1979), 5–8.

JOHN BEER ON "LONDON" AS OPEN TO INTERPRETATION

[John Beer wrote *Blake's Humanism* and *Blake's Visionary Universe* and the essays "Blake, Coleridge and Wordsworth: Some Cross Currents and Parallels, 1789–1805" and "Influence and Independence in Blake". In this essay, Beer shows how Blake's poems can be interpreted on several different levels. Beer believes that the poem defies complacent interpretation.]

One's judgement in so delicately balanced a matter is likely to be swayed by one's sense of Blake's work as a whole at this time; it is from my own sense of it, certainly, that I question whether 'London' is *primarily* an 'apocalyptic' poem—at least in the common sense of the word. Edward Thompson argues it to be a virtue of such an interpretation that in making all the final images ones of commerce and of forthcoming doom it allows the poem to 'shut like a box'. With most eighteenth-century poets this would indeed be a virtue, but I am not sure that the same applies to Blake. For his poems have a habit (irritating when first encountered) of springing open again just when one thinks one has closed them—almost as if they were the work of a man who believed that a poem which shut like a box might also be a prison. Despite my own strong interest in the structures of ideas in Blake's poems, and the undoubted existence of an apocalyptic note in them, I also feel that the interpretations which are most faithful to their total effect are those which (like Dr Glen's) preserve an antinomian quality in the very meanings of the poems themselves.

There is on the other hand a price to be paid for such openness; for there will be times when we simply do not have the means to decide between possible interpretations. To take up one of Dr Glen's own claims, it is hard to see how we can be sure that the observer in 'London' who 'marks' the marks in the faces that he sees is thereby demonstrating an abstracting and mechanical mental narrowness of his own. The obsessive focussing of his gaze on those of others might be a sign of extreme and generous humanity rather than its opposite.

One answer to such problems, of course, is to regard them as demonstrating the hermeneutic versatility of Blake's poetry and adding to their richness; but that will not quite do either. There is something about the very intensity of his writing in such places which urges the reader to interpret it directly. On any particular occasion, therefore, it is likely that the reader will make up his or her mind one way or the other. What our discussion seems to demonstrate is that in certain cases the reading of a single word may be decisive in fixing the balance of interpretation: in so short a poem as 'London' the leading significance assigned to 'mark' is enough to swing the dominant tone of the whole.

Investigation of a single word in Blake can prove equally fruitful elsewhere—and especially so if it turns out to unravel a concise shorthand for some complicated train of thought and imagery. Another word which repays study is 'intellectual', as in the line 'A tear is an intellectual thing'. Although that line no doubt makes gratifying reading to sentimental theoreticians, it stands out strangely in Blake—particularly since the specific use of 'intellectual' as we have come to know it belongs to a later period. At this point, however, we can turn to Kathleen Raine, who points out that 'intellect' is a term which appears in Thomas Taylor's translations from the Platonists. She quotes, for example, a passage which begins as follows: 'Intellect indeed is beautiful, and the most beautiful of all things, being situated in a pure light and in a pure splendor, and comprehending in itself the nature of beings, of which indeed this our beautiful material world is but the shadow and image . . . '[44] A passage such as this certainly seems to be echoed by Blake, who, after speaking in *Jerusalem* of Imagination as 'the real & eternal World of which this Vegetable Universe is but a faint shadow',[45] goes on to inquire whether the Holy Ghost is any other than an 'Intellectual Fountain'.[46] Shortly afterwards he describes God as 'the intellectual fountain of Humanity'.[47] The coupling of the two favourite neo-Platonist concepts of 'intellect' and 'fountain' as attributes of the divine provides strong evidence for the existence of a direct influence.

Although these are comparatively late statements, moreover, they seem to reflect an earlier formulation of Blake's, for his earlier uses of 'intellect' also carry a charge which suggests that he thinks of it in dynamic terms, as an in-dwelling power—directly linked, as in Plotinus, to a realm of intellect which transcends the world of generation and death.

NOTES

44. Kathleen Raine, *Blake and Tradition* (2 vols, London, 1969), vol. II, p. 195, citing T. Taylor, *Five Books of Plotinus* (1794), pp. 243–4.

45. *Jerusalem* 77 (Raine, *Tradition*).

46. *Jerusalem* 77 (not in Raine).

47. *Jerusalem* 91.11 (not in Raine).

—John Beer, "Influence and Independence in Blake." In *Interpreting Blake*, ed. M. Phillips (Cambridge: Cambridge University Press, 1979), 220–222.

[Stewart Crehan is a Professor of English at the Manchester Metropolitan University in the United Kingdom. He has written *Blake in Context* and *Nature's Excess: Physiocratic Theory and Romanticism*. In this essay, Crehan explains that Blake paints a bleak picture of life in "London". He believes that religion, politics, and marriage all act negatively on the people of the city. While the poem is politically and socially critical, "London" also *describes* the life of the citizens.]

Though clearly a poem of protest, *London* transcends the rhetoric of contemporary radical protest in several important ways. First of all, the 'I' of the poem does not overtly accuse, but simply wanders through 'each charter'd street', passively recording what he sees and hears. The lack of any overt crusading outburst makes the signs of social misery ('Marks of weakness, marks of woe') seem all the more inescapable. Their presence overwhelms us. The monotonous repetitions of the first two stanzas ('charter'd', 'marks' and 'every'), together with the Johnsonian generality of the 'hapless Soldier's' and 'the youthful Harlot's', register an ineluctable—that is, *social* condition. The perception of a doomed and rotten society is *heard* rather than seen: what we see we can choose not to see, but what we hear is less easily shut out. Individual moral outrage or denunciation is redundant in a poem whose shock effect lies in the objective force of the human images themselves.

This is, of course, a mark of Blake's success as a poet. In Book VII of *The Prelude*, Wordsworth describes how as an idle resident he walked London's streets, observing, with wonder and awe, the 'endless stream of men and moving things'. Recording a never-ending spectacle, the poet suggests a multitudinous yet confusingly trivial variety of human specimens, but it is interesting to note that the three central figures in Blake's poem—the chimney sweeper, the soldier and the harlot—do not occur anywhere in Wordsworth's compendious observations. Although they loom large in Blake's urban landscape, they were not *empirically* the obvious figures to choose.

Contemporary social protest often added the threat of divine vengeance, but in Blake's poem no heavenly judgment is needed, since both the judgment and the threat come from within the urban system itself. Biblical, apocalyptic allusions are present, but the workings of society revealed in the poem have an apocalyptic logic of their own. The voice of protest has been objectified. The millenarian Richard Brothers wrote of London:

> her streets are full of Prostitutes, and many of her houses are full of *crimes*; it is for such exceeding great wickedness that St. John *spiritually* calls *London* in his chapter (Revelation 11:8) by the name of *Sodom . . . . For my designation is, and the commands of God to me are, that I shall walk through the great thoroughfare-street of the city, to pronounce his judgements, and declare them irrevocable . . .*

And a follower of Brothers, Thomas Taylor, addressed the 'opulent possessors of property' as follows:

> Know you, that the cries of the Widow, Fatherless Children, and the defenceless oppressed Poor, are come up unto the ears of the Lord of *Hosts*. He is ready to undertake their cause: and if you repent not of your evil deeds, *He will consume you*, with the breath of his mouth.

In Blake's *London* the possibility of that kind of judgment and repentance is excluded, since what is exposed is not 'crimes', 'wickedness' and 'evil deeds', but a *whole social system*.

The images in the last two stanzas show how established religion is bound up with exploitation, politics is bound up with war, and marriage is bound up with prostitution. The chimney sweeper's cry, instead of coming 'up unto the ears of the Lords of *Hosts*', casts a pall over every 'black'ning Church', whose blackness, caused by the smoke from the chimneys that the sweeps clean, and darkening, instead of brightening, the lives of those who live under it, makes the target—here, the guilty clergy's hypocritical concern—concretely visible. The 'hapless Soldier's sigh' is not heard by God, but becomes visible as blood running down 'Palace walls'. The image both exposes and indicts the 'hapless' soldier's *true* enemy, which is not Republican France, but king, parliament and archbishop who, from the safety of their respective palaces, urge poor labouring men to die for their country, fighting the foreigner. The image, however, is ambiguous, and as such contains a prophetic warning: the blood could one day be the oppressor's. Finally, it is not the breath of the

Lord that consumes, but the 'Harlot's curse'. The curse is syphilis, whose contagion indiscriminately blinds the new-born infant and turns the marriage bed into a 'hearse'. But the plagues with which the harlot blights the 'Marriage hearse' are also symbolic. They are a *verbal* curse on the confining hypocrisy of legalised, monogamous marriage itself. (. . .)

London is a poem of political and social protest; it is also a poem about London, and the experience of living in London. The freedom to wander the streets is shown to be illusory when a mercantile system that annuls the rights of the majority is so complete that even the Thames is 'charter'd'. By his 'marking' the speaker relates to others at a less than human level, in a vast city where all are strangers. As E. P. Thompson has shown, the word 'mark' would have had a number of associations for Blake's readers. Revelation 13:17 speaks of 'the mark of the beast' on those who buy and sell. London's streets were full of the cries of street-sellers, in which Blake's speaker hears only 'mind-forg'd manacles'. The freedom to buy and sell shackles 'every Man'—*including* the speaker—in a de-personalising system based, not on genuine human contact, but on the exchange of goods and money. There is no possibility within the speaker's mode of perception, trapped as he is in this impersonal system, of hearing a street-cry, say, as a poetic utterance, an assertion of something human behind the figure of the seller. (To illustrate this point, a 'flower man' during the French wars was heard to cry: 'All alive! all alive! Growing, blowing; all alive!' and a blind man, accompanied by his wife and children, cried his mats and brooms in rhyming couplets, ending: 'So I in darkness am oblig'd to go;/To sell my goods I wander to and fro.') Blake's speaker, as a 'free' individual wandering the streets, marks every other 'free' individual not as a person, but as a face with 'marks' in it. Into every face he meets he also draws the marks of his *own* weakness and woe; he tellingly picks out, with a deceptive lack of conscious choice, those most degraded by the system, a system in which the labour-power of infants and the charms of female children could be bought in the streets.

The urban experience in *London* is not only alienating, but is one in which growing violence and incipient revolt are strongly felt. Though the speaker makes no direct accusation, rising protest is heard in the tone of voice, from 'I wander' to 'But most . . .'. The poem moves from a kind of weary aimlessness (suggested by the long vowel sounds in 'charter'd' and 'mark(s)') to the shocked exclamations ('How . . .' etc.) of stanza three, with its emphatic trochaic rhythm, to the verbal violence of the climactic final stanza, with its rasping 'curse', 'Blasts', 'blights' and 'plagues'. The poem is a violent crescendo of verbal sounds and meanings, held within a tightly disciplined form. Its hyperbolic extremism is an imaginative revelation of a whole urban process, as the poem moves from alienation and distress to inarticulate violence.

> —Stewart Crehan, *Blake in Context* (Dublin: Gill and Macmillan Humanities Press, 1984), 72–79.

GAVIN EDWARDS ON REPETITION IN "LONDON"

[Gavin Edwards has taught at the Universities of Sydney and Gothenburg and at St. David's University College. He has published *George Crabbe's Poetry on Border Land* and *George Crabbe: Selected Poems*. In this essay, "Repeating the Same Dull Sound", Edwards probes the meanings of the words *charter'd*, *ban*, *curse*, and *mark* within the context of "London".]

'London' (and I am taking the word as the title of the poem beneath it rather than the caption of the picture above it) obviously involves a sequence of voices heard in the street, over and over again. But its interest is wider than that; it includes a whole range of acts of vocalisation and scription: sighs and charters and marks as well as curses and bans. Four of Blake's words are particularly interesting in the present context: 'charter'd', 'ban', 'curse', and 'mark'. They are all words that, in other grammatical forms, can act as performatives. Briefly, performative utterance are utterances that themselves perform the actions to which they refer. Thus:

> Lawyers when talking about legal instruments will distinguish the preamble, which recites the circumstances in which a transaction is effected, and on the other hand the operative part—the part of it which actually performs the legal act which it is the purpose of

the instrument to perform. . . . 'I give and bequeath my watch to my brother' would be an operative clause and is a performative utterance.

This example Is pertinent for a number of reasons. First, it demonstrates that written discourse (a charter, for instance) can involve performative utterances. Second, 'I give and bequeath x to y' is clearly a formula, a repeated phrase, and it needs to be if the instrument is to be legally binding. Furthermore such ritual performatives are clearly always of particular significance where conventional relationships are being established in a conventional context—such as the fixing of rights of property and inheritance (charters for the incorporation of companies or towns), social contracts between rulers and ruled (Magna Carta), articles of apprenticeship (such as those signed by James Blake and James Basire), marriage ceremonies (the 'I do' of William Blake and Catherine Boucher, the 'I declare you man and wife' of the parson), and baptisms (I name this child . . .'). Such situations provide most of J. L. Austin's examples, and Blake's poem is overwhelmingly concerned with the overlapping areas of Church, Law, property, generational inheritance, and marriage.

As for the words themselves, 'I curse' would be a performative, as would 'I ban', and the poem also alludes to the banns of marriage, which gives us the parson's 'I publish the banns of marriage between . . . .' Charters are legal instruments that have to involve performative utterances, though I have not come across a charter in which the word itself is used performatively (as in 'I/We charter'). Finally, 'mark' is a special case to which I shall return.

Evidently these words in Blake's poem ('charter'd', 'ban', and curse') are not themselves performative. But as nouns or participial adjectives, they are what Barbara Johnson has called 'deactivated performatives'. And the particular force that seems to animate them in the poem derives, I believe, from their direct reference to situations in which those same words help to constitute performative utterances. Austin points out that in performative words there is an '*asymmetry* of a systematic kind [with respect to] other persons and tenses of the *very same word*'. For instance, 'I curse you' is a performative utterance, whereas 'he curses you', like 'I hear you', is not since it refers to an event independent of the referring utterance.

The words in the poem—'charter'd', 'ban', and curse'—derive at least some of their force from how they embody this asymmetry. They refer to conditions in the world outside the poem, but how they so refer is determined by the fact that, as deactivated performatives, they are also existentially linked to actual performative utterances. The poem's words actually do bear the operative power of performative utterance within themselves, in a congealed form. Consequently the social conditions to which the words refer, as well as the words themselves, appear as the marks of acts performed another grammatical form by the utterance of those very same words. Those social conditions are represented therefore not so much as facts but as *faits accomplis*. The word 'charter'd' bears repetition in the poem because of the force to which it is linked. These performatives are uttered in Churches and law Courts where their force is inseparable from the fact that they have been said before and will be said again.

Blake's use of these words tends to confirm another of Austin's contentions, that performative utterances depend for their plausibility on at least a tacit acceptance by the interlocutor of the conventions involved in their use. Indeed to describe the situations of their use as conventional implies as much. Most of Austin's examples, and these three words from the poem, are concerned with human power relationships. And the poem's use of these words suggests that to be at the receiving end of performative utterances of this kind is to be more than labelled: it is to take the label to heart, to assume it as one's identity, even unwittingly. The religious and juridical act of christening could be taken as exemplary in this respect. It is an act of labelling imposed arbitrarily on the basis of our father's name and our parents' wishes that we take as the sign of our personal identity. The achievement of the poem is to register such acts as the imposition of arbitrary labels that are nevertheless not external to those who receive them: as marks inscribed by authority that are also signs of an inward condition, marks 'Of weakness and of woe'.

There is only one actual performative in Blake's poem, and that is 'I . . . mark'. Of course, one sense of the verb *mark* in the poem is 'to observe'. In this sense the word reports on the poet's action as he walks the streets and is not performative. But since the same word used as a noun in 'Marks of weakness, marks of woe' refers to physical alterations of the human body, and since the practice in which the poet is actually engaged involves inscription on paper and the subsequent biting of the copper plate by acid to reveal the letters in relief, then surely there is also a reference in 'I . . . mark' to itself. In so far as 'I . . . mark' means 'I observe', the relationship established between the marked faces and the poet who marks them is of the fatally reflexive kind that Heather Glen has so accurately described. Blake, she argues, shows us what it means to be both at odds with and yet conditioned by one's cultural ethos:

> The relentless, restricting categorising which stamps the Thames as surely as it does the streets is like his own mode of relating to the world. He may 'wander' freely enough, but he can only 'mark' one repetitive set of 'marks' in all the different faces before him.

And this is still the case if one admits the sense of 'mark' as an act of perception involving a registering or noting of what is perceived. The writer and reader implied by that registering are still caught within the same kind of specular relationship, in a poetic utterance that presents itself as an unmediated survey of the reality it simply repeats. But in so far as 'I . . . mark' refers also to itself as an act of inscription, all those mirror-relationships are fissured, marked, rendered problematic. The best way to explain this effect is in terms of the different forms of the present tense that the ways of reading 'I . . . mark' imply. The poem employs a generalising present tense, one that describes 'what I am doing' but 'what I do' (repeatedly). But in so far as 'I not . . . mark' is self-referential, it introduces the present tense of 'what I am doing,' and this has a number of consequences. First, it links the poetic utterance existentially to the writing self, in a way that can be associated with the existential link that I have argued for between the deactivated performatives and the actual performative utterances to which they refer. But, second, this self is not the unitary entity that its grammatical name, 'first person singular', suggests; it is not the anterior source of the utterance. 'I . . . mark' is self-referential both in the sense that it refers to the self and in the sense that it refers to itself. 'I . . . mark' describes me in the act of scription, but it also *is* the act of scription. Consequently the present it reveals is not a moment but a movement, and there is no governing Subject but a continual differentiation in which the subject of the act of writing and the subject of what is written never finally coincide or separate.

> —Gavin Edwards, "Repeating the Same Dull Round," *New Casebooks: William Blake*, ed. David Punter (New York, St. Martin's Press, 1996), 108–120.

HAROLD BLOOM ON WANDERING THROUGH "LONDON"

[Harold Bloom is Sterling Professor of the Humanities at Yale University. He has written more than 16 books and edited more than 30 anthologies, including *Blake's Apocalypse, William Blake's* Songs of Innocence and of Experience, and *Modern Critical Views: William Blake*. In this writing, he compares Blake to a Biblical prophet who wanders through the city creating verse full of words worth studying.]

Blake begins: "I wander thro' each charter'd street," and so we begin also, with that wandering and that chartering, in order to define that "I." Is it an Ezekiel-like prophet, or someone whose role and function are altogether different? To "wander" is to have no destination and no purpose. A biblical prophet may wander when he is cast out into the desert, when his voice becomes a voice in the wilderness, but he does not wander when he goes through the midst of the city, through the midst of Jerusalem the City of God. There, his inspired voice always has purpose, and his inspired feet always have destination. Blake knew all this, and knew it with a knowing beyond our knowing. When he begins by saying that he *wanders* in London, his Jerusalem, his City of God, then he begins also by saying "I am not Ezekiel, I am not a prophet, I am too fearful to be the prophet I ought to be, *I am hid.*"

"Charter'd" is as crucial as "wander." The word is even richer with multiple significations and rhetorical ironics, in this context, than criticism so far has noticed. Here are the relevant shades of meaning: There is certainly a reference to London having been created originally as a city by a charter to that effect. As certainly, there is an ironic allusion to the celebrated political slogan: "the chartered rights of Englishmen." More subtly, as we will see, there is a reference to *writing*, because to be chartered is to be written, since a charter is a written grant from authority, or a document outlining a process of incorporation. In addition, there are the commercial notions of hiring, or leasing, indeed of binding or covenanting, always crucial in a prophetic context. Most important, I think, in this poem that turns upon a mark of salvation or destruction, is the accepted meaning that to be chartered is to be awarded a special privilege or a particular immunity, which is established by a written document. Finally, there is a meaning opposed to "wandering," which is charting or mapping, so as to preclude mere wandering. The streets of London are chartered, Blake says, and so he adds is the Thames, and we can surmise that for Blake, the adjective is primarily negative in its ironics, since his manuscript drafts show that he substituted the word "chartered" for the word "dirty" in both instances.

—Harold Bloom, "Blake and Revisionism," *William Blake's Songs* of Innocence and of Experience, ed. Harold Bloom (New York, Chelsea House, 1987), 55–58.

CRITICAL ANALYSIS OF

"The Mental Traveller"

Like many of Blake's poems, "The Mental Traveller" challenges scholars. Some try to compare the symbolism to other Blake poems; others believe "The Mental Traveller" cannot be compared to the rest of Blake's work. It is tempting, too, to interpret the poem as an autobiographical piece; in any case, "The Mental Traveller" recounts the travels of an emotionally troubled man through life, unable to connect with the people who mean the most to him.

The work starts with the description of a journey; the narrator is traveling the earth. He comes across the birth of a child and decides to follow this person through the course of his life. While the birth is celebrated, there are tears associated with its beginning. Perhaps the parents have a hard life, or the child was not conceived in love. The tears could spring from the pain of childbirth, or perhaps the pain of knowledge: the knowledge of the hard life ahead for the newborn baby. The child is given to a "woman old" to be cared for. At this point, Blake's prose becomes Biblical: the images in the next stanza evoke the suffering of Christ. The child suffers as Christ did, crowned with thorns and wounded on the hands and feet as if nailed to a cross.

Dark images continue to plague the boy. It appears that the "woman old", the child's caretaker, enjoys his suffering; she "lives upon his shrieks and cries" and "grows young as he grows old". True, as a child matures, the worries about its raising are transformed into new anxieties; true also, the additional responsibilities can weigh heavier on—and thereby age—the child. But is the old woman really parasitic, or does Blake mean to imply that caring for a child can be a nourishing or even a regenerative process?

The poem seems to describe an unhealthy mother-child relationship; this relationship becomes a pattern in the subject's life. The boy becomes a man. He replaces the "woman old" with a partner of some sort. Because he feels he was not raised in a loving manner, he treats the new woman in his life as he was treated as a child.

The narrator tells us about the sadness in the life of the subject. He appears to be going through life as if already dead. He is wealthy but unhappy. While he does not mention regrets, he does seem to have unfulfilled wishes. His suffering continues to grow. "They are his meat they are his drink." His misery feeds itself, growing larger as life goes on. The narrator seems to think that his suffering as an adult, as it was in his infancy, is enjoyed by others.

There seems to be a new happiness in his life with the birth of the boy's daughter. Emotionally, he appears to be incapable of one aspect of parenting: love. He feels unworthy to give his daughter the love she is looking for. As she grows up, she finds love in others, and her Father has lost another opportunity in his life. This inspires a change:

> He wanders weeping far away
> Until some other take him in

Self-pity has the subject, and apparently someone else, feeling sorry for him. To feel better, he takes a lover. The physical expression of love changes his world. "The flat Earth becomes a ball." The sun and moon pull away. He loses all sense of time, with no reminders of day and night, and only his lover exists:

> A desart vast without a bound
> And nothing left to eat or drink
> And a dark desert all around

The desert may represent the place in his life where love can grow. It is a space of extremes: like agony and bliss, peace and anger, love and hatred. Beautiful things can blossom and grow in the desert, but they are short-lived.

The subject of the work feels the love he has found rejuvenates him. He is enjoying the emotions that come from finding a partner. They get to know each other.

> And on the desart wild they both
> Wander in terror & dismay

Apparently, what she has learned about the speaker is too much for her to handle. Instead of working out their problems, she chooses another course of action:

> Like the wild stag she flees away
> Her fear plants a thicket wild

> While he pursues her night & day
> By various arts of Love beguild

Clearly, she is trying to distance herself from the Speaker; she tries to prevent the success of their union by withholding her heart. The subject of the poem finds himself desperate to continue the relationship and tries to win her back. His lack of success in recreating the love they shared devastates him. After being spurned, he returns to his old way of thinking, but this time the "desert" of his soul becomes "Labyrinths of wayward Love"—a maze that he alone can navigate. This transformation, while protecting his heart, will impede the next affair, and whereas before he was dysfunctional, now he is a broken man.

A pathetic creature now heads into the later years of his life. He has become like an infant again, needing care. The end of his life is similar to its beginning: the woman he has taken as his lover has become a "weeping Woman Old." Weeping perhaps, for her lost youth, or the loss of her life with her lover. It appears that he is trying to reach out to others in his advanced age, having become very aware of the passage of time. He opens again:

> To all who in the desart roam
> Till many a City there is Built
> And many a pleasant Shepherds home

Relationships allow the speaker a measure of peace, instead of death in the desert of his soul. He builds a foundation of friendship with others.

When death approaches, though, fear grips the speaker. Those close to him abandon him in his hour of need—this too recalls the Bible, specifically Christ in the garden. Those who reach out to the dying man fear the worst and find that his decaying physical state has made his company unpleasant. He dies alone. All around him have left, with one notable exception: the old woman. Thus Blake returns to the beginning of the poem; in death, the subject of the poem faces the same future as at his birth.

"The Mental Traveller"

NORTHROP FRYE ON "THE MENTAL TRAVELLER" AS A LIFE JOURNEY

[Northrop Frye taught at the University of Toronto and was a well-known and respected literary theorist. His major works include *Fearful Symmetry*, *Anatomy of Criticism*, and *The Great Code*. This writing examines the work and compares it to a man's life: infancy, adulthood, death and rebirth.]

In traditional Christian symbolism, God the Creator is symbolically male, and all human souls, whether of men or of women, are creatures, and therefore symbolically female. In Blake, the real man is creating man; hence all human beings, men or women, are symbolically male. The symbolic female in Blake is what we call nature, and has four relations to humanity, depending on the quality of the vision. In the world of death, or Satan, which Blake calls Ulro, the human body is completely absorbed in the body of nature—a 'dark Hermaphrodite', as Blake says in *The Gates of Paradise*. In the ordinary world of experience, which Blake calls Generation, the relation of humanity to nature is that of subject to object. In the usually frustrated and suppressed world of sexual desire, which Blake calls Beulah, the relation is that of lover to beloved, and in the purely imaginative or creative state, called Eden, the relation is that of creator to creature. In the first two worlds, nature is a remote and tantalizing 'female will'; in the last two she is an 'emanation'. Human women are associated with this female nature only when in their behaviour they dramatize its characteristics. The relations between man and nature in the individual and historical cycles are different, and are summarized in *The Mental Traveller*, a poem as closely related to the cyclical symbolism of twentieth-century poetry as Keats's *La Belle Dame Sans Merci* is to pre-Raphaelite poetry.

The Mental Traveller traces the life of a 'Boy' from infancy through manhood to death and rebirth. This Boy represents humanity, and consequently the cycle he goes through can be read either individually and psychologically, or socially and historically. The latter reading is easier and closer to the centre of gravity of what Blake is talking about. The poem traces a cycle, but the cycle differs from that of the single vision in that the emphasis is thrown on rebirth and return instead of on death. A female principle, nature, cycles in contrary motion against the Boy, growing young as he grows old and vice versa, and producing four phases that we may call son and mother, husband and wife, father and daughter, ghost (Blake's 'spectre'), and ghostly bride (Blake's 'emanation'). Having set them down, we next observe that not one of these relations is genuine: the mother is not really a mother, nor the daughter really a daughter, and similarly with the other states. The 'Woman Old', the nurse who takes charge of the Boy, is Mother Nature, whom Blake calls Tirzah, and who ensures that everyone enters this world in the mutilated and imprisoned form of the physical body. The sacrifice of the dying god repeats this symbolism, which is why the birth of the Boy also contains the symbols of the Passion (we should compare this part of *The Mental Traveller* with the end of *Jerusalem 67*).

As the Boy grows up, he subdues a part of nature to his will, which thereupon becomes his mistress: a stage represented elsewhere in the Preludium to *America*. As the cycle completes what Yeats would call its first gyre, we reach the opposite pole of a 'Female Babe' whom, like the newborn Boy, no one dares touch. This female represents the 'emanation' or accumulated form of what the Boy has created in his life. If she were a real daughter and not a changeling, she would be the Boy's own permanent creation, as Jerusalem is the daughter of Albion, 'a City, yet a Woman'; and with the appearance of such a permanent creation, the cycle of nature would come to an end. But in this world all creative achievements are inherited by someone else and are lost to their creator. This failure to take possession of one's own deepest experience is the theme of *The Crystal Cabinet* (by comparing the imagery of this latter poem with *Jerusalem 70* we discover that the Female Babe's name, in this context, is Rahab). The Boy, now an old man at the point of death, acquires, like the aged King David, another 'maiden' to keep his body warm on his death-bed. He is now in the desert or wilderness, which symbolizes the end of a cycle, and his maiden is

Lilith, the bride of the desert, whom Blake elsewhere calls the Shadowy Female. The Boy as an old man is in an 'alastor' relation to her: he ought to be still making the kind of creative effort that produced the Female Babe, but instead he keeps seeking his 'emanation' or created form outside himself, until eventually the desert is partially renewed by his efforts, he comes again into the place of seed, and the cycle starts once more.

—Northrop Frye, "The Keys to the Gates," *Modern Critical Views: William Blake*, ed. Harold Bloom (New York: Chelsea House, 1985), 56–57.

JOHN H. SUTHERLAND ON IRONY AND OPPRESSION

[John H. Sutherland was a Professor at the University of Pennsylvania and edited *Colby Quarterly*. In this essay, Sutherland examines the reasons behind Blake's ironic tone and the influence of man and spirit on the work.]

In 'The Mental Traveller', Blake is intensely, and ironically, aware of the value of suffering to the tyrant: 'They [groans and sighs] are his meat, they are his drink.' Blake is purposely ironic as he records the aged Shadow's generosity with this kind of riches: 'He feeds the Beggar & the Poor.' His door is 'for ever open' to those who are vulnerable to human pain. Moreover, this is a give-and-take arrangement. The groans and sighs seem to be deliberately conceived as ambivalent: they are produced by poor, oppressed mortals for the delectation of the tyrant Shadow, and they are distributed as food (or in lieu of food) to the poor and oppressed by the Shadow.

This is the normal end of the Orc cycle. The next step would be the breakdown of the static and corrupt establishment, a falling back into a period of gestation, and then the rebirth of the young spirit to repeat the process. However, as a mental traveller with creative vision, Blake did not see man as inexorably caught by such a pagan nightmare. Stanza eleven records what can happen if people in the cottage (i.e., on earth) find, to the aged Shadow's grief, some way of exercising their creative powers:

His [the Shadow's] grief is their eternal joy;
They make the roofs & walls [heaven and earth] to ring;
Till from the fire on the hearth
A little Female Babe does spring.

The Female Babe springs from fire—symbolically the source of energy and inspiration. She is described in stanza twelve as being 'all of solid fire / And gems & gold'—so awe-inspiring that no one dares to touch her. The aged Shadow (in stanza thirteen called the 'aged Host') fears and hates this splendid product of man's creative powers. He feeds on man's grief; it makes perfect sense that the creative imagination, which can free man from grief, is the source of his grief. In terms of the ideas symbolized, the exact, mechanical, and limiting principles in the universe must have something to limit in order to exist at all. Thus, when applied to man, they exist, literally, because of man's grief. When men find their way through to some source of creative energy, they free themselves and bring grief to that power which previously had oppressed them.

In stanza thirteen, the Female Babe is presented as an archetypal spirit closely akin to a muse. She is described as coming 'to the Man she loves' (the artist, and perhaps the mystic and the saint); together, the man and the Female Babe drive out 'the aged Host, / A Beggar at another's door'. (Here 'the Man she loves' seems to be primarily the human individual, who can, through creative inspiration, free himself from the dead hand of Urizen; however, it may also refer to mankind as a whole, since the fate of the aged Host after he loses his kingdom is described in symbolic terms which can apply at any level. He could be losing control of one man and one man's world; he could also be losing control of the whole planet, as mankind now knows it through its fallen senses.)

Once Urizen has been driven out, he tries, more and more desperately, to find some person or thing to impose himself on. He finally wins a 'Maiden':

And to allay his freezing Age
The Poor Man takes her in his arms;
The Cottage fades before his sight,
The Garden & its lovely Charms.

The maiden seems to represent materialism and the world of the fallen senses. The aged Shadow, now appropriately called the 'Poor

Man', embraces materialism as a last resort, and very naturally falls out of the world of archetypes in Eternity into the limited world which is the lowest common denominator of sensory apprehension. There is nothing said here of vortexes, in the sense Blake used the term when explaining the nature of infinity in *Milton*; however, it is quite clear that the aged Shadow has passed through the vortexes of the material world and now sees things from a point of view similar to that of a person on this earth. In Eternity, Earth was but a cottage, and its inhabitants were all together. To the fallen senses, Earth seems a vast ball, and its inhabitants appear to be separated by great distances:

> The Guests are scatter'd thro' the land,
> For the Eye altering alters all;
> The Senses roll themselves in fear,
> And the flat Earth becomes a Ball;
>
> The stars, sun, Moon, all shrink away,
> A desert vast without a bound,
> And nothing left to eat or drink,
> And a dark desert all around.

Although Blake does not say so directly anywhere in the poem, it seems likely that the maiden the cast-out aged Host turns to is a frustrated female Babe, grown older without finding 'the Man she loves'. Just as it was natural for the male Babe, Orc, to cease to represent energy and revolt, so it is natural for a female Babe—once a muse—to degenerate into a coquette and sensualist. It is noteworthy that sensuality and the artifices of physical and emotional love have an entirely different effect on her than they do on the aged Shadow. His part is to pursue the fleeting pleasure of simple indulgence, and this, very naturally, makes an infant of him. Her part is to lead him through 'Labyrinths of wayward Love' by means of 'various arts of Love & Hate'. Just as naturally, this makes an old woman of her.

There is violence and inaccuracy in the giving of abstract equivalents for these figures at any of the stages of their development. However, if one allows for that, it seems illuminating to consider the direct proportion here suggested: the female Babe is to the Maiden (who becomes the weeping Woman Old), as the male Babe is to the bleeding youth (who becomes the aged Host). This is to say: creative imagination is to sexual love (which ages into the cruelty of 'Mother' Nature), as creative energy is to physical construction (which ages into the conservative principle of tyranny and repression).

The principal weakness of this proportion is that it suggests static balance while Blake is talking about cyclical flux. The relationship of the two figures in the poem follows the general line of the relationship in the proportion, but it is dynamic, and constantly shifting, as is necessary for the continuation of their cyclical existence. Near the end of the poem, the conservative principle reverts again to infancy as it is betrayed and teased in the world of the senses. The cycle is completed when 'he becomes a wayward Babe, / And she a weeping Woman Old'. At the same time they return from out the fallen world into Eternity as 'The Sun & Stars are nearer roll'd'. (Note that most of these relationships are supported directly by the text of the poem. The hypothetical connection between the female Babe and the Maiden only adds detail to the structure.)

The return to Eternity does not involve physical travelling—it is brought about by an improvement in the sense organs. In *The Marriage of Heaven and Hell* Blake explains the process this way:

If the doors of perception were cleansed every thing would appear to man as it is, infinite.
For man has closed himself up, till he sees all things thro' narrow chinks of his cavern.

In 'The Mental Traveller', the improvement in apprehension seems to come at least partly because of the improvement in environment. Paradoxically, although the fall seems to have been partially due to fear ('The Senses roll themselves in fear, / And the flat Earth becomes a Ball'), the planting of the desert is also partly due to fear ('Like the wild Stag she flees away, / Her fear plants many a thicket wild'). Those thickets which are not due to fear are the result of a kind of love which is very closely related to fear: ' . . . the wide desart planted o'er / With Labyrinths of wayward Love, / Where roam the Lion, Wolf & Boar.' Thus, that which helped cause the fall from Eternity is an indirect cause of the temporary regaining of Eternity.

These thickets of passion are very like those described in greater detail in some of the *Songs of Experience* ('A Poison Tree, 'The Garden of Love', 'My Pretty Rose-Tree'). They are far from being happy products, but they are—like the jungle—symbols of simple fertility. As such, they are a necessary background to the development of love, and to the growth of cities and civilization. Love and civilization represented creative achievement to Blake; he thought of them as important stages on the road to seeing things (at least partially) in their eternal forms. Thus, at the very time that the thickets of love have made a Babe of the aged Host, and a Woman Old of the Maiden, they have made an environment in which 'many a Lover wanders', and which helps bring about the return to Eternity.

—John H. Sutherland, "Blake's Mental Traveller," *Critics on Blake: Readings in Literary Criticism*, ed. Judith O'Neill (Coral Gables: University of Miami Press, 1970), 74–77.

David Wagenknecht on Blake's History

[David Wagenknecht was an Associate Professor of English at Boston University and editor of *Studies in Romanticism*. He wrote *Blake's Night: William Blake and the Idea of Pastoral*. This passage illustrates how "The Mental Traveller" is a poetic timeline of Blake's life; according to Wagenknecht, this work is not the first time this theme has appeared.]

Blake seemed to know that "ontogeny recapitulates phylogeny." The worm is born a child, and, in sinister parody of Milton's "Nativity Hymn," "a shriek ran thro' Eternity: / And a paralytic stroke" (E78). Orc's appearance is disturbing enough that the Eternals secure the stakes of the Tent, thereby preventing Los from beholding Eternity any more. Orc's post-partum career is just as ambiguous. Orc grows, and his father correspondingly grows jealous, forging link by painful link a chain of jealousy, with which Orc is chained, like Prometheus, to a rock "beneath Urizens deathful shadow" (E79). Then,

> 5. The dead heard the voice of the child
> And began to awake from sleep
> All things. heard the voice of the child
> And began to awake to life.
> (E79)

the passage suggests Adonis, Orpheus, and the triumph of *eros* over *thanatos*. Whether resurrection in this case is a happy event is less certain.

In other important instances Blake muffles ambiguity and anxiety by presenting the career of Vala in terms of a historical cycle which seems tantalizingly to progress but which, eventually, like the drift of Thel's imagery, loops back on itself. His ultimate presentation of such a cycle, as I have noted, is in "The Mental Traveller" (which he never published) in which four distinct stages of cycle are distinguished but seen to drive each other like meshed cogwheels. The end of the fourth stage can be taken to illustrate how Blake could apply his doubts about Generation to historical analysis. It corresponds generally to the second stage of the process as related by Luvah in *Vala/The Four Zoas*, where pursuit of Nature as elusive female (in fact a chimera) and construction of a labyrinth is mistaken for the constructive power of civilization and progress toward enlightenment:

> Till the wide desart planted oer
> With Labyrinths of wayward Love
> Where roams the Lion Wolf & Boar
> Till he becomes a wayward Babe
> And she a weeping Woman Old
> Then many a Lover wanders here
> The Sun & Stars are nearer rolld
>
> The trees bring forth sweet Extacy
> To all who in the desart roam
> Till many a City there is Built
> And many a pleasant Shepherds home
> (E477)

The last two lines suggest Blake's England, with its urban life and proliferation of country retreats, and the reference to the "wayward Babe" should suggest Lyca, whose poems also bore reference to the poet's own time. But Blake's sense of history is complex, for although it may have been Newton who helped to roll the sun and stars nearer, "the trees bring[ing] forth sweet Extacy" suggest. the Fall for "all who in the desart roam." Apparently Blake is describing a case where city planning (or, more generally, culture) recapitulates phylogeny. And again Blake compounds the Old Adam and the New, for immediately we are told,

But when they find the frowning Babe
Terror strikes thro the region wide
They cry the Babe the Babe is Born
And flee away on Every side
(E477)

The Babe is saviour perhaps only in the odd Blakean sense that (like Milton's Satan) he withers Nature, but the sense of natural law is strong enough to overpower even such upstarts, and—terrifying or not—the "frowning Babe" is nailed down upon the rock by "a Woman Old."

—David Wagenknecht, Blake's Night: William Blake and the Idea of Pastoral (Cambridge: Harvard University Press, 1973), 169–171.

HAROLD BLOOM ON "THE MENTAL TRAVELLER" AS STANDING ALONE

[Harold Bloom is a Sterling Professor of the Humanities at Yale University. He has written more than 16 books and edited more than 30 anthologies, including *Blake's Apocalypse, William Blake's* Songs of Innocence and of Experience, and *Modern Critical Views: William Blake.* This essay points out that the work does not follow the pattern of Blake's other poems. Bloom shows us how the work is able to affect readers and fit into the pattern of life.]

What counts most about *The Mental Traveller* is its openness and vigor; the marching rhythms and easy diction suggest that Blake is attempting his own kind of lyrical ballad, and consciously wants to give the reader a story so direct and passionate in its grim ironies that the quite overt moral will ring out unmistakably in the poem's last line: "And all is done as I have told." The Orc cycle, the withering of desire into restraint, is the theme of *The Mental Traveller* as it was of much of *The Four Zoas*, but to say that *The Mental Traveller* is "about" the Orc cycle is to schematize too quickly. A descriptive account of the poem ought to emphasize the large movements of its drama; the symbolic vision will emerge of itself, for that is the poem's greatness. The reader is compelled by the poem's very starkness to solve the relationship between repetitiveness in the poem's events and the pattern of similar ironic repetitiveness in the reader's own life.

The poem's title clearly refers to the "I" who chants its events, and whose wondering observation of the cycle of natural life determines the poem's fresh and startled tone. The poem is a report of a strange and distorted planet given by a being who has stumbled upon it and cannot altogether believe the horrors he has seen. His nervous vibrancy is felt in every stanza, as he strives to communicate to us, the poem's implied audience, the grim marvels of an existence that by the poem's largest irony, is already our own:

> I travel'd thro' a Land of Men,
> A Land of Men & Women too,
> And heard & saw such dreadful things
> As cold Earth wanderers never knew.

This Traveller, who is presumably one of Blake's unfallen Eternals, moves mentally through our world, expecting that a Land of Men will yield him human images. But he sees that the human image is already divided; the Sexes have sprung from shame and pride, and it is a Land of Men and Women too. He hears, sees and also *knows* what the cold wanderers of Earth hear and see also, but cannot apprehend as knowledge, which is one of the poem's major points. If you cannot learn from experience, then you must suffer it over and over again. In the next stanza the Mental Traveler contrasts the fallen process of birth with the Eternal progression reached through the liberating strife of contraries:

> For there the Babe is born in joy
> That was begotten in dire woe;
> Just as we Reap in joy the fruit
> Which we in bitter tears did sow.

The sexual meeting of fallen man and woman seems a "dire work" to this being, who compares it to the intellectual warfare of Eternity. The fruit of Eternity is a liberated creation, but the fruit of earthly intercourse is a Babe who suffers the fate of the Norse Titan Loki, of Jesus, and of Prometheus, three incarnations of Luvah as a suffering Orc, or simply three dying man-gods:

And if the Babe is born a Boy
He's given to a Woman Old,
Who nails him down upon a rock,
Catches his shrieks in cups of gold.

She binds iron thorns around his head,
She pierces both his hands & feet,
She cuts his heart out at his side
To make it feel both cold & heat.

Loki, punished for his part in the slaying of Balder, suffered precisely as the Babe does in the first of these stanzas, and the allusions to Jesus and Prometheus are unmistakable in the second. But, more directly, this is *any* new human child, and *every* new human impulse, idea, creation, fresh life of all kinds. An old woman, a nurse or foster mother, nature itself, receives this new imaginative force, and nails him down to the rock of material existence, the fallen body and its limitations. The Babe's shrieks are precious to her, as Loki's are to the gods, for they are evidences of her continued dominion over man. She makes a martyr lest she have to contend with a fully human antagonist. The iron thorns are not only an allusion to Jesus, but also to Blake's ironclad Spectre of Urthona, the crippled, anxiety-ridden temporal will of man. The pierced hands and feet betoken the impairment of man by nature, and the exposed heart is the depraved natural heart, bereft of the affective powers of Eternity. For death feeds upon life, nature on the human, the Old Woman on the Babe:

Her fingers number every Nerve,
Just as a Miser counts his gold;
She lives upon his shrieks & cries,
And she grows young as he grows old.

This is horror, the genuine obscenity of a vampire will, natural and female, nourishing itself on the only wealth we have, the substance of our hope, the possibility manifested in a human child. But the horror is ours; the poem's speaker maintains his grimly level tone, as he continues to describe a world so different from his own.

It begins to be clear that the poem has two cycles moving in it, in opposite directions, and out of phase with one another. The female or natural cycle is moving backwards, the male or human cycle forward: "And she grows young as he grows old." At mid-phase they meet, and enact a scene akin to the "Preludium" of *America*, where Orc rends up his manacles and possesses the nameless female who had cared for him:

> Till he becomes a bleeding youth,
> And she becomes a Virgin bright;
> Then he rends up his Manacles
> And binds her down for his delight.
>
> He plants himself in all her Nerves,
> Just as a Husbandman his mould;
> And she becomes his dwelling place
> And Garden fruitful seventy fold.

—Harold Bloom, *Blake's Apocalypse: A Study in Poetic Argument* (Ithaca: Cornell University Press, 1963), 289–292.

ALICIA OSTRIKER ON SOUND AND STRUCTURE

[Alicia Ostriker is a Professor of English at Rutgers University and a poet and critic. She is the author of *Vision and Verse in William Blake* and the editor of *William Blake: The Complete Poems*. Her poetry has been published as *Songs* and *A Dream of Springtime*. This work describes the ways in which alliteration helps to form the vivid images of Blake's symbolism.]

When he leaves proper names and explicit moralizing behind, as in 'My Spectre around me," "The Golden Net," "The Mental Traveller," and—almost—in "The Grey Monk," he achieves finer results. These semi-dramatic narratives all rely on a self-consistent symbolic structure in the same way that Blake's prophecies do; that is, they make no compromise with, popular understanding. Let the reader beware, now that Blake has entered the maze of his system and shut the door behind him. An outsider will receive only minimal assistance from the conventional meanings of some of Blake's key symbols.[5]

"The Mental Traveller," most finished and best constructed of this group, employs meter with an almost passionate monotony which betrays all along what the last lines will declare plainly: that a cyclic futility poisons the veins of human history. We do not quite realize this until the conclusion. The ironic *seeming* significance of "such dreadful things" as the narrative relates is produced by the startling imagery, by the packed, declarative syntactical structure which makes almost every stanza appear a completed "episode," and by the individual fingering of his lines. Despite confinement to iambs, with a few trochaic inversions, almost no anapests, and only occasional emphatic pauses, Blake achieves sufficient variety by degrees of accenting and placing of slight pauses. (. . .)

The sound patterns, combining alliteration and a rich vowel range, give additional vividness. Note how "Catches his shrieks with cups of gold" modulates from harsh, to high, to deep and cold vowel. But this vividness is spurious, fantastic, like a surrealist landscape or a painting by De Chirico, where distinct detail only enhances the pervasive unreality, and one is uncomfortably conscious of the empty spaces. Blake was describing the tedium of abortive change in a world without apocalypse, a theme he expanded for the epics dealing with what Northrop Frye calls the "Orc cycle."[5]

The other poems in this group are strongest when, like "The Mental Traveller," they keep within the iamb–trochee gamut. They are weakest when they lapse loosely into anapests without structural or rhetorical justification. Nothing about them outrages the ear, for the poet has not lost his competence. Few things ravish it, either, for he has lost some of his interest in making every syllable of his lyrics count. Except for "The Mental Traveller," these poems are interesting mainly for their attempt to condense prophetic matter into lyric scope.

NOTE

5. *Fearful Symmetry, a Study of William Blake* (Princeton, 1947), pp. 207–35.

—Alicia Ostriker, *Vision and Verse in William Blake* (Madison: The University of Wisconsin Press, 1965), 94–99.

[Victor Paananen wrote *William Blake*, and *William Blake: Updated Edition* and edited *British Marxist Criticism*. In this analysis of the work, Paananen shows how nature, or human nature to be exact, is the story behind "The Mental Traveller". It is an idea that influences many of Blake's poems.]

The most challenging of the cyclic poems is the difficult "The Mental Traveller," in which the repetitions seem to be the most mocking. The speaker of the poem is a "mental traveller" who will offer a visionary account of life in our fallen world, the world of Generation ("A Land of Men & Women too"). We are told how Nature—Tirzah in Blake's myth—repeats the binding of Orc in every human life, dictating the acceptance of the suffering within nature that Jesus knew at the crucifixion and forming in the process the suffering natural heart:

> She binds iron thorns upon his head,
> She pierces both his hands & feet,
> She cuts his heart out at his side
> To make it feel both cold & heat. (*CW*. 425)

It is this heart that leads human beings first to sexual love and then to the practice of the fallen virtue of pity, a virtue only possible when we *accept* an inadequate world. Pity is often institutionalized into charitable organizations:

> An aged Shadow, soon he fades,
> Wand'ring round an Earthly Cot,
> Full filled all with gems & gold
> Which he by industry had got.
>
> And these are the gems of the Human Soul,
> The rubies & pearls of a lovesick eye,
> The Countless gold of the akeing heart,
> The martyr's groan & the lover's sigh.

They are his meat, they are his drink;
He feeds the Beggar & the Poor
And the wayfaring Traveller:
For ever open is his door. (*CW.* 425)

In the same way that political liberalism is based on an acceptance of capitalism as "natural," liberal institutions such as this elderly man embodies are based on an acceptance of the world as it appears. The ideological foundations of such philanthropy cannot endure the birth of a new concept such as that represented by 'A little Female Babe":

And she is all of solid fire
And gems & gold, that none his hand
Dares stretch to touch her Baby form,
Or wrap her in his swaddling-band. (*CW.* 425)

The infant Orc, victim of Nature, has turned into the ancient Urizen: he is no longer a creative "male" who can recognize the revolutionary "female" creation that should be the result of his own effort to change the world but instead frightens him. In the world of Generation—the world of separate subject and object, characterized by the existence of the sexes—"male" and "female" are in perpetual conflict, as Los and Enitharmon have already shown in the mythic works.

The reaction that the Urizenic figure brings into being, an analogue to political reaction, destroys even the charitable institutions to leave us face to face with the desert of ratio perception:

The Senses roll themselves in fear,
And the flat Earth becomes a Ball;

The stars, sun, Moon, all shrink away,
A desart vast without a bound.
And nothing left to eat or drink,
And a dark desart all around. (*CW.* 426)

Yet, on the other hand, a new idea has come into being that has in fact jolted the male figure out of his liberalism and into a conservatism that is unacceptable for the continuation of human life ("nothing left to eat or drink"). The Urizenic figure thus casts off his ideological baggage to become rapidly more youthful until he is again the infant Orc who is not yet victim to the ancient abstraction "Nature":

he becomes a wayward Babe,
And she a weeping Woman Old.
Then many a Lover wanders here;
The Sun & Stars are nearer roll'd. (*CW.* 426)

The world becomes momentarily more human as lovers walk in
freedom again and as the stars cease to be quite as remote as they
usually are. But, because the "female" is restrictive nature again,
reaction is inevitable:

They cry "The Babe! the Babe is Born!"
And flee away on Every side.

For who dare touch the frowning form,
His arm is wither'd to its root;
Lions, Boars, Wolves, all howling flee,
And every Tree does shed its fruit.

And none can touch that frowning form,
Except it be a Woman Old;
She nails him down upon the Rock,
And all is done as I have its told. (*CW.* 427)

No hope of satisfaction—or of a human life at all—is possible if one
continues to accept "nature" as both given and determining. Political
change is a source of hope only when it is based on a philosophic
understanding that permits an active intervention into that world that
seems fixed. If political faiths are based on an acceptance of nature
as given in the natural cycles, and therefore also based on an
acceptance through empirical epistemology of both a commodified
world and a commodified humanity, they too will fail. Our happiness
is to be found only when we can shatter all the enclosing wheels of
nature and history, put an end to alienation and the division of labor,
and establish a fully human existence.

As William Adams has very well explained, in the future that
Marx envisions after the end of private property, "The eye has
become a *human* eye, just as its *object* has become a social, *human*
object, made by man for man." Blake would make the same
projection, calling this life Eternity, as experienced by our Divine
Humanity.

—Victor N. Paananen, *William Blake: Updated Edition* (New York:
Twayne, 1996), 120–123.

[Nicholas Williams is an Associate Professor at Indiana
University. He has written *Ideology and Utopia in the
Poetry of William Blake* and many essays on the Romantics.
In this essay, Williams finds that "The Mental Traveller" has
a 'poetic voice like no other' of Blake's works. He feels the
poem is unusually written and takes a different path than
Blake's usual imagery.]

"The Mental Traveller" is an odd production not only for its
appearing in this context of manuscript verse, but for the way it
rehearses some of the major themes of his poetry without recourse
to the mythological apparatus for which he is best (and most
fearsomely) known. Even without this apparatus, the startling
newness of Blake's vision is apparent in the double story of a "Babe"
given to a "Woman Old," who gets progressively older as she
becomes young, only to end once again as an infant, a "frowning
form" whose fate recapitulates the poem's opening:

> And none can touch that frowning form
> Except it be a Woman Old
> She nails him down upon the Rock
> And all is done as I have its told.   (101–5, E486)

The elements of this text which mark it as "Blakean," and which
have encouraged some to see Blake as a creator distinct from his
historical setting, are the seeming freedom from traditional frames
of reference and the unusual vividness of the stark imagery. If this is
an allegory, and as much is suggested by Blake's tone of normative
explanation ("And if the Babe is born a Boy / He's given to a Woman
Old" [9, 10]), then it is an allegory like no other, whose ties to
established cultural codes (the Christian story, classical myth, etc.)
are at best oblique. Despite attempts to translate it by reference to
these codes or to Blake's own "mythology," the poem retains the
characteristics of an interpretive scandal, and seems always fresh in
its capacity to resist easy codification.

But if the poem carries with it a shock of newness, a sensation
that here is a poetic voice like no other, such a feeling rests uneasily

beside the subject matter of the poem itself. That tone of normative certainty which gives to Blake's poems their sense of urgency and importance, also lends to them a claustrophobic sense of limitation, of already determined futures and of indefinite repetition. That tale told by the Mental Traveller is one of mental bondage and violence, the Old Woman's crucifixion of the Babe mirrored by his later revenge:

> Till he becomes a bleeding youth
> And she becomes a Virgin bright
> Then he rends up his Manacles
> And binds her down for his delight   (21–4, E484)

Indeed, the persistent mirroring in the poem—the boy "Babe" of the opening and the "Female Babe" of the middle, the Old woman and the man "blind & age-bent" (55), as well as the parallel bindings at the poem core—all suggest that this world's inhabitants are forced to repeat the same limited repertoire of actions again and again. (. . .)

What are we to make of such an anomaly, such a discontinuity between a seeming originality of insight and the apparent denial of any originality whatsoever? One option, of course, is to attempt to translate the allegory, to figure out what Blake "means" by this strange narrative, most often by interpreting his characters as the equivalents of general concepts, of external Nature (the Woman) or Humanity (the Man). But in addition to not respecting the nonspecific terms of Blake's poem, such an approach risks overlooking a central element of its powerful effect. It attempts, in a sense, to overstep the boundaries that Blake evocatively establishes in the poem's opening stanza:

> I travld thro' a Land of Men
> A Land of Men & Women too
> And heard & saw such dreadful things
> As cold Earth wanderers never knew. (1–4, E483)

We might take the speaker here to mean that he is reporting on a non-Earthly scene in the lines that follow, that he is a kind of proto-spaceman recording extra-terrestrial happenings for the home planet (such science-fictional frameworks are not inappropriate for the author of "Air Island in the Moon"). But what is more likely is a logical opposition of the "Mental Traveller" of the title and the

"Earth wanderers" of line 4, distinguishing between two modes of travel rather than two destinations. What the lines suggest, in other words, is an even more striking anomaly at work in the poem, a contradiction between the uniformity of event described ("all is done as I have told") and the complete lack of knowledge of those events on the part of those who are forced to suffer through them. One might, of course, simply take this as an assertion of poetic vision, in the transhistorical sense, making a claim for the poet's ability to see beyond the time-bound, mundane conceptions of the "Earth wanderers" to the effulgent realities of transcendent truth. By such an interpretation, the poem's opening stanza represents a strong instance of what might be called the "aesthetic ideology" or, even more specifically, the "Romantic ideology," in its privileging of the ideal over the real, the mental over the physical, the intellectual over the corporeal. But what complicates this picture is the fact that what the Mental Traveller sees is a vision of extreme corporeality, or, to put it another way, what the poem develops is itself a theory of ideology. If the opening stanza proposes an opposition between what the Mental Traveller can hear and see and what the Earthly wanderers can know, we have yet to consider the later description of the perceptual abilities of the "Guests" who invade the old man's cottage:

> The Guests are scatter'd thro' the land
> For the Eye altering alters all
> The Senses roll themselves in fear
> And the flat Earth becomes a Ball. (61–4, E485)

Juxtaposed with the magisterial eye of the Mental Traveller, whose vision seems to be raised above the physical, we have this very material, sense-bound "Eye" whose power, or lack of power, effectively creates the world around it. (. . .)

The Mental Traveller tells stories of limited sensual abilities, paralyzed consciousness, but the very ability to tell these stories presumes a point beyond their purview, a point from which they can be "known" and, in some cases, changed. I take as a founding presupposition of what follows that Blake's goal in most of his work is a kind of traveling, a kind of change, but that rather than be satisfied with mere "mental traveling," the path of this career is a search for the route to that total engagement of human capacities, in both individual and social forms, which he called "Eden." The path to Eden will not he found by an evasion of ideology, by a mentalized ideal vision of easeful love (what Blake called *Beulah*), but instead by a harsh imagining and reimagining of the ideological world. It is in this sense of a hard-won and reimagined vision of the ideological world that I will call Blake's Edenic visions "utopian," distinguishing this use of the word from its other, less politically viable meanings.

—Nicholas M. Williams, *Ideology and Utopia in the Poetry of William Blake* (Cambridge: Cambridge University Press, 1998), 1–5.

CRITICAL ANALYSIS OF

"The Crystal Cabinet"

The essays that follow attempt to untangle the web of images and messages in Blake's "The Crystal Cabinet." One critic finds allusions to alchemy in the verses; while another traces similarities between "The Crystal Cabinet" and other Blake poems. A third sees the work as a warning about sex. If the mark of a great work of art is its capacity to reflect each member of its audience in a way different from the reflection of each other member, then "The Crystal Cabinet" meets the criterion.

As the poem starts, its speaker claims to be happy, dancing in the wild. He meets a woman and ends up locked up in her cabinet, though he seems to have put up little fight if any at all. The image of entrapment is common in Blake's poems. This time, it seems he has entered the state of love without reservation. He becomes entranced—"[l]ockd up with a golden key", a key whose strength comes not from its composition but from its beauty—and, at this point in the poem, does not struggle against his imprisonment. Indeed, he becomes upset when his confinement ends. The romantic union has opened up a new world to the speaker:

> . . . within it opens into a World
> And a little lovely Moony Night

The night brings the soft, flattering glow of moonlight, which casts a gentle spell on everything in its path; the speaker is enchanted. Under the spell of his love, the speaker's vision itself seems altered:

> Another England there I saw
> Another London with its Tower
> Another Thames & other Hills
> And another pleasant Surrey Bower

His emotions influence his perceptions. The speaker doesn't say he's found a *better* England, just a *different* one. Other writings make it clear that Blake had much to say about the state of politics and economy in his London. Perhaps the "lovely Moony Night" shows London in an unjustifiably favorable light, or distorted views of the river Thames. Or does the speaker's love blind him to the problems of a newly industrialized London?

After a small series of *another*, Blake adds another *another*: another maiden. Is this the same woman, seen in "another" way—"Another Maiden like herself"—or is it someone new?

Next, Blake makes mention of the first of three instances of *threefold* in "The Crystal Cabinet"—a triple vision that will become his undoing. He continues:

> O what a smile a threefold Smile
> Filld me that like a flame I burnd
> I bent to Kiss the lovely Maid
> And found a Threefold Kiss returnd

In this verse are the other two instances of the word *threefold*—three in total as a seemingly obvious reference to the Holy Trinity. Although his beliefs did not conform to those of any established religion, did Blake mention the word three times for some spiritual purpose? The line "Threefold each in the other closed" recalls the Catholic and Anglican tenet of the three forms of God in one being. Is the lovely maiden the speaker kisses the Virgin Mary? She's described as "[t]ranslucent lovely shining clear", similar to the Catholic or Anglican idea of the Mother of God. Is the kiss the speaker gave to the "maiden" returned by the Father, the Son, and the Holy Spirit? The speaker "strives to seize the inmost form," as if looking for understanding or perhaps searching for religious enlightenment. In his work, Blake often questioned Protestant religious teachings, and he tended to satirize religious beliefs. Perhaps "The Crystal Cabinet" represents another example of Blake's skeptical approach to organized religion.

The word "weeping" will also make a triple appearance in "The Crystal Cabinet." The speaker weeps after the "Crystal Cabinet" is broken when the speaker tries to seize its core. His passion leads to loss. Blake uses the word "burst" to describe the destruction of the Cabinet; the triple mirror is shattered. This is a violent eruption, causing irreparable damage, and the speaker weeps not for a broken heart but for a broken life. Indeed, it is because the speaker now will have to begin life anew that Blake transforms him into an infant. A crying woman, pale and weak after surviving the destruction of "The Crystal Cabinet", enters the picture.

The last two lines of the poem are amazingly clear:

And in the outward Air again
I filld with woes the passing Wind

The speaker is in a fog, as if intoxicated or clearing his head after a bad dream. "The Crystal Cabinet" ends with a bit of sadness: love is lost, a life is starting over, and the speaker is surrounded by his own woe.

"The Crystal Cabinet"

IRENE H. CHAYES ON THE INFLUENCE OF MYTH

[Irene H. Chayes taught at the University of Maryland. She
has written extensively about the Romantic Poets, including
the essays "Some Versions of the Antique" and
"Michelangelo's 'The Last Judgment'". In this passage,
Chayes shows how several of Blake's poems demonstrate
the legacy of Greek and Roman mythology. She examines
"The Crystal Cabinet" in the context of the story of Cupid
and Psyche.]

How do source studies contribute to an understanding of Blake's
"visionary forms"? What is the relation of traditional iconography to
the imagery in both his poetry and his designs? In his case, it is
especially true that the work is to be trusted more than the man, and
in spite of his strictures on "the classics" his work itself shows that
Blake was sufficiently a product of his age to draw on the traditional
Greek and Roman myths as well as on more esoteric material for the
complex purposes of his two parallel arts. Behind the eccentric
proper names and the composite episodes of the epics we can
recognize from time to time the familiar figures of Demeter and
Persephone, Zeus and Prometheus, Apollo, Poseidon, or
Hephaestus. Among the designs, there may be the surprise effect of
a fall of Lucifer that is also the fall of Phaëthon, as on plate 5 of *The
Marriage of Heaven and Hell*, or, on the last plate of *Europe: A
Prophecy*, a revision of Aeneas' flight from Troy, in which the dead
Creusa seems to be substituted for the aged Anchises. It is true that
these are usually only fleeting echoes or allusions with a limited
function, and the very familiarity of the originals undoubtedly left
little for Blake to do by way of adaptation or variation that would
have been an adequate challenge to his imagination. There was one
classical myth, however, whose special history and associations set
it apart from those that had become hackneyed through overuse by
the time Blake began work.

This was the myth of Cupid and Psyche, which is best known as an interpolated story, or parable, or fable, in *The Metamorphoses* (IV, 28–VI, 24), popularly called *The Golden Ass*, by Apuleius of Madaura. Apuleius, in turn, had received his material from a tradition of myth and ritual which may have originated in the Orphic Mysteries and which has survived mainly in the iconography of a variety of minor antique works of art—funerary reliefs, statuary, frescoes, mosaics, engraved gems. In a third tradition, the writers on mythology in later ages, from Fulgentius in the sixth century, to Boccaccio, to the speculative mythographers of the eighteenth and early nineteenth centuries, preserved a continuity of their own in discussions of Cupid and Psyche, both together and separately, as independent mythic figures. By the time of the Romantics, when there was a new interest in Cupid and Psyche among major and minor writers alike,[1] all three traditions were available and in varying combinations affected the way in which the myth was understood, even when Apuleius' literary version continued to be the main source. Through his training in art and his professional work as an engraver, as well as through his more conventional literary interests, Blake was in a position to regard the two figures and the myth from more than one standpoint and in more than one context of meaning. The evidence is that he did precisely that, and from what he saw chose motifs for both his poetry and his designs which furnished him with considerably more than a means of appealing to what his audience already knew or of acknowledging that "the classics" sometimes had anticipated his own characters and situations. Although the results remain purely Blake's own, to trace the separate motifs back to their probable origins and forward in new variations and combinations is to learn much that is valuable about the workings of his imagination, both verbal and visual, and about the relation of his two arts to each other. (. . .)

In *The Crystal Cabinet*, from a later time, the male speaker undergoes a fall like Psyche's when he tries to exceed the limits set on his enjoyment of the miniature world within the Cabinet; in striving to seize "the inmost Form," he breaks the Crystal Cabinet (as an image, a variant of Psyche's magic palace) and finds himself exiled and weeping "upon the Wild." Even *The Sick Rose* is ambiguous in its relation to the chapters in *The Golden Ass*. The uncommon use of the second person, the curious tone, with its hint of *Schadenfreude*, and the reference to the nocturnal visits of the corrupting "invisible worm" recall not the voice of the narrator but the slanders of the jealous sisters, who tell Psyche that her unseen husband is actually a monstrous, poisonous snake and who eventually destroy themselves in their successive efforts to replace her in Cupid's favor. (. . .)

Male and female contend for power and possession in *The Crystal Cabinet*, which begins with the Maiden as pursuer and the dancing male speaker as her captive, a reversal of earlier roles until he becomes possessive in turn. In *The Mental Traveller*, where the myth is most fully realized, the archetypal man and woman alternate in a rising and falling pattern of conflict, disparity, and frustration which coincides with a highly complex, cyclical pattern of human and cosmic ages.[23] *The Fly* is a step toward both, linking them with "How sweet I roam'd" of long before by way of the motif of butterfly- and bird-hunting. Logically and chronologically, however, the evolution of Blake's sexual myth is not complete without two other poems, which have not yet been mentioned. Like *The Fly* they belong to *Songs of Innocence and of Experience*, and their relation to the iconography of Cupid and Psyche also involves their relation to each other.

NOTES

1. Thomas Taylor's prose translation of Apuleius' fable (1795) was followed by adaptations in verse by Mary Tighe (1795) and Hudson Gurney (1799); Mary Shelley began a translation of her own in 1817 but left it unfinished. Erasmus Darwin and Thomas Moore as well as Keats and Coleridge wrote poems with specific allusions to the myth; references to Cupid and Psyche both together and separately recur among Coleridge's published and unpublished prose. On sources of the myth in literature and art that were available to the Romantics, see E. H. Haight, *Apuleius and His Influence*, reprinted New York, 1963, chs. 6 and 7, and Ian Jack, *Keats and the Mirror of Art*, Oxford, 1967, ch. 12.

Work on this essay was assisted in part by grants from the American Council of Learned Societies and the American Philosophical Society. For information and courtesies, I am indebted also to the Prints Division of the New York Public Library, the Department of Prints and Drawings of the British Museum, and P. & D. Colnaghi & Co., Ltd., of London.

23. On *The Mental Traveller*, see my "Plato's *Statesman* Myth in Shelley and Blake," *Comparative Literature*, XIII (1961), 361–368.

—Irene H. Chayes, "The Presence of Cupid and Psyche," *Blake's Visionary Forms Dramatic*, ed. David V. Erdman and John E. Grant (Princeton: Princeton University Press, 1970), 214–217.

ROBERT E. SIMMONS ON BLAKE'S BALANCE

[Robert E. Simmons is an Associate Professor of English at York University's Glendon Campus. He has written *The Language of Literature: A Stylistic Introduction to Literature*. This passage takes a look at the mathematical precision with which Blake crafted his words. Simmons says "The Crystal Cabinet" is almost scientific in its symbolism.]

The second point of emphasis is the usefulness of a symmetrical model" for describing, and thus reading, Blake. Northrop Frye uses a "diabolical" and "divine" symmetry for elucidating Blake's imagery, but I would stress the symmetrical forms of his structures—and even his grammar—as well. The *Songs of Innocence and of Experience* and *The Marriage of Heaven and Hell* are obvious examples. *The Tyger, The Crystal Cabinet, The Mental Traveller* all end where they begin, with the difference of a mirror image. The last plate of *Job* reflects the first—with a significant difference. *America, Europe,* and the "Asia" and "Africa" sections of *The Son of Los* combine to form a symmetrical structure related to the four continents. *The Book of Los* (four chapters) and *The Book of Ahania* (five chapters) frame *The Book of Urizen* (nine chapters) to form another symmetrical structure.

The similarity of the structure of *The Four Zoas* (nine nights) to *Urizen* (nine chapters) might also be remarked upon, together with the fact that material from *Urizen* recurs in all the long prophecies. The orientation, or directional, symbolism of *Urizen* also recurs, suggesting that the investigation of structural symmetries in the late works may well be profitable.

But the concept of symmetry not only may be applied broadly to other Blake works, it may also be used in much greater depth, with more precision and delicacy, on individual works than has been possible in the limited space of this essay. Such an exact application and description may reveal that Blake's "system" of symbolism is even more systematic and extensive than it has been thought to be. This suggestion, if it is confirmed, would fit in well both with the basic concept of the fallen world as symmetrical and cyclical and with Blake's very extensive knowledge and use of contemporary science as revealed in his imagery.[11]

The Crystal Cabinet illustrates these points in miniature. The poem turns on the notion of a "three-fold" symmetry. The speaker enters a "crystal" and sees three women where once was one. He tries to seize the "inmost form," or fix the exact, mathematical shape of these images, and breaks the crystal instead, thus revealing their threefold symmetry as illusory. But symmetry, the exact, repeated life in the crystal world, now seems to him delightful, and he is filled with woe to find himself outside once more with what seems to him to be the anguished chaos of a nature impossible to organize into such pretty, repeated shapes. The final point of this analysis is that in the science of crystallography, or the analysis of the symmetries of crystals, "three-fold" symmetry (the same terminology is used) is one of the commonest forms and is illustrated by rock quartz.

NOTES

11 J.H.H.: It might be well, at the same time, to take into account the tradition of *chiasmus*, a basic form of Hebrew poetry, where the climax is in the middle, and where one moves in the following fashion:

This form explains much in Blake and is somewhat truer both to his tradition and to his own manner of proceeding than is the overworked term "cyclical."

—Robert E. Simmons, "Urizen: The Symmetry of Fear," *Blake's Visionary Forms Dramatic*, ed. David V. Erdman and John E. Grant (Princeton: Princeton University Press, 1970), 167–169.

[Hazard Adams is a Professor Emeritus in Comparative Literature at the University of Washington. His publications include *Blake and Yeats: The Contrary Vision*, *William Blake: A Reading of the Shorter Poems*, and the novels *Many Pretty Toys* and *Home*. Here, Adams explains the images of Innocence in "The Crystal Cabinet" and offers several interpretations of the work.]

The speaker recalls a state of unrestrained innocence represented by his dance. He has discovered there a shape-changing female, who performs an act analogous to the crucifixion of Orc in "The Mental Traveller." The difference is that the maiden has seduced the speaker. Distinctions rigidly adhered to in "The Mental Traveller" are somewhat blurred or collapsed, for this speaker is not certain about the experience himself. Tirzah the mother and Rahab the seductress are not distinguished from one another, for the speaker is time-borne. Tirzah is forgotten, though her action is described as accomplished by Rahab. In considering the sexual aspect of the symbolism—cabinet, lock, key, etc.—we move at once to encompass a simple Freudian reading and see that the clearly sexual imagery is symbolic of a meaning larger than itself; for the female is the whole of the outer world as well as her sexual self. In the speaker's eyes, the two actions of "The Mental Traveller"—capture by the earth mother and rape of the virgin bright—are suddenly one and the same in remembrance. We can think of the capture of the speaker as following the last part of the cycle of "The Mental Traveller," if we assume that the speaker *remembers* the female not as a Tirzah but only as a Rahab.

What we discover is that the male has been contained by the female rather than encompassing her. The crystal cabinet is an area just short of vision, holding within itself all the possibilities of vision. It is clearly related to what Blake calls Beulah, the state of threefold vision, passive pleasure, and moony nights. But Beulah is part of the fallen world here, the uppermost area below Eden; it is a part of the triple form which is nature—Beulah, Generation, and Ulro. In some respects it is a gate, but a gate has two directions and no one is capable of staying in the gate itself for long, just as each moment in fallen time must disappear.

The action in Beulah is very nearly successful, but the danger of Beulah is its seductivity and the tendency of the passive dreamer of moony nights to abstract his vision from himself and assume its separate existence. The result is the familiar fall into multiplicity, seen here as an infinite regress in which the vision of the "other," really the self, becomes a series of mirrors or a crystal. The "other maiden" whom the speaker sees is really, then, the same maiden split into a triple form by the process of "reflecting" upon an outer world. The number three in Blake is associated with a vision of nature halfway between the chaotic area of Generation and the fourfold vision of Eden. In Beulah, if man externalizes the threefold maiden and thus fails to encompass within his own imaginative form the triple world of nature which she represents, he falls into Ulro.

We notice, then, that within Beulah a choice is presented to the speaker. He may expand his vision to encompass all of a beautiful spiritual England, all of London—a city like the woman that Albion finally marries in *Jerusalem*. The vision is that of London *within* England (Albion). To make this choice would be to expand inward in that paradoxical Blakean fashion that always puts Eden at the still point of the circle and Ulro at the circumference. Or to put it another way:

What is Above is Within, for every-thing in Eternity is translucent:
The Circumference is Within: Without, is formed the Selfish Center
(*Jerusalem*, Ch. 3, K 709)

Such an interpretation seems to contradict the preceding statement, but the terms are simply reversed. The real or upright world is really the world of mental forms without material substance. The true expansion to the infinite circumference of God, which is traditionally both everywhere and nowhere in measurable space, is therefore within, while to assume oneself the center of the material universe is to enclose oneself in the Urizenic cave of the ego. The speaker, in other words, can proceed from the sexual to the human vision, where nature is no longer a surrounding physical existence but a city within the spirit.

The second choice, or perhaps we should call it temptation, is to turn around, or inside out, and instead of looking within look without. Then the true England becomes a triple female named Rahab, an indefinite cyclical conception or crystal mirror suggesting something beyond herself (translucent) but actually reflecting a debased image of the self. Although this mirror woman can return a kiss, to grasp her is as impossible as to reach successfully through a mirror. The result is, of course, a shattering of the glass itself.

Now any bursting forth might, on first appearance, suggest an apocalyptic assertion of new life similar to breaking the shell of the traditional cosmic egg or ascension from the grave. But if we accept Blake's paradoxical spatial imagery we see that the true rebirth does not come from breaking out of the crystal cabinet into another merely larger cyclical world. Such action might go on indefinitely, the infinite space of modern physical science providing the wanderer with shell after shell to be broken through. Instead, proper vision lies in an inward expansion in which one's own spiritual body surrounds that "other England" within the grain of sand. Any violent reading out destroys the vision. From within the crystal cabinet the translucence, which is really reflection, suggests a tantalizing possibility of something beyond the perceivable or visionary fact. And yet with that translucence smashed, the reflection of the self is apparently translucent again, on a larger more remote concave surface. This should be the spiritual lesson of modern science.

We may note the paradoxical aspects of the crystal cabinet by observing that it is related, on the one hand, to the "crystal house" of *Europe*, where it is a symbol of the cyclical enclosure of fallen time and space ruled over by a nature-goddess, Enitharmon:

> Then Enitharmon saw her sons & daughters rise around.
> Like pearly clouds they meet together in the crystal house.
> (*Europe*, "A Prophecy")

On the other hand, it has aspects of "the grain of sand" image in Blake which appears frequently to illustrate the paradox of inward visionary expansion. The grain of sand appears most prominently in the following places: at the beginning of "Auguries of Innocence," where it is used to express the identity of macrocosm and microcosm (that which is above is that which is within).

NOTE

Citations marked "K" are to Geoffrey Keynes, ed., *The Complete Writings of William Blake* (London: The Nonesuch Press; New York: Random House, 1957). References are to page numbers. [ED.]

> —Hazard Adams, "The Crystal Cabinet and the Golden Net," *Blake: A Collection of Critical Essays*, ed. Northrop Frye (Englewood Cliffs: Prentice Hall, Inc., 1966), 80–83.

VICTOR N. PAANANEN ON SEXUAL EXPRESSION

[Victor N. Paananen wrote *William Blake*, and *William Blake: Updated Edition* and edited *British Marxist Criticism*. In this essay, Paananen explores Blake's warning about sex—that sexual love does not provide escape from life's problems.]

If "The Mental Traveller" offers hints about the impossibility of success in political endeavor that is based on an acceptance of the world as it is currently constituted, "The Crystal Cabinet" offers a clear warning against a reliance on sexuality to lead to transcendence of our condition. In this poem, the speaker encounters a maiden who seems to be able to offer film entry into a realm that is, somehow, this physical world repeated in a finer tone:

> She put me into her Cabinet
> And Lock'd me up with a golden Key.
>
> The Cabinet is form'd of Gold
> And Pearl & Crystal shining bright,
> And within it opens into a World
> And a little lovely Moony Night.
>
> Another England there I saw,
> Another London with its Tower,
> Another Thames & other Hills,
> And another pleasant Surrey Bower. (*CW*, 429)

If he could possess her here, he might possess a Keatsian—or
Lawrentian—eternity:

> like a flame I burn'd;
> I bent to Kiss the lovely Maid,
> And found a Threefold Kiss return'd. (*CW*, 429)

But his attempt must fall, and his actual subservience to nature is
instead emphasized:

> I strove to seize the inmost Form
> With ardor fierce & hands of flame,
> But burst the Crystal Cabinet,
> And like a Weeping Babe became—
>
> A weeping Babe upon the wild,
> And Weeping Woman pale reclin'd,
> And in the outward air again
> I fill'd with woes the passing Wind. (*CW*, 429–30)

Nature is to be destroyed or transcended. Its "inmost Form,"
could it be grasped, provides only the grounds for the despair of the
empiricist. If we do not strive for change that is fundamental and
rounded in a philosophy and theology that breaks with the
empiricists, neither politics nor sexual love hold out hope for the
satisfaction of human needs.

These three cyclical poems offer it particularly effective
statement against trusting either political reformism or indeed a
sexual "revolution," such as we were said to have experienced in the
1960s, as a final answer. Blake was, like Marx, a thoroughgoing
revolutionary in his quest for an end to human alienation, and for
Blake that goal meant pressing onto the full freedom of Eternity.
"Many persons, such as Paine & Voltaire, with some of the Ancient
Greeks, say: 'we will not converse concerning Good & Evil; we will
live in Paradise & Liberty.' You may do so in Spirit, but not in the
Mortal Body as you pretend, till after the Last Judgment" (*CW*,
615–16). (It is worth recalling here Blake's explanation of how the
Last Judgment occurs: "Whenever an Individual rejects Error &
Embraces Truth, a Last Judgment passes upon that Individual" [*CW*,
613].) The trap that Paine or Voltaire creates in accepting nature is
reproduced in the structure of these poems: nature's seasons or the
alternations of revolution and counterrevolution enclose us, as do the

tiger patterns of repeated incident and repeated phrase. The three cyclical poems, taken together with the other manuscript poems, remind us that, even though Blake chose to devote much of his career to works on a larger scale, he had few peers in the fusion of form and meaning in the short poem.

> —Victor N. Paananen, *William Blake: Updated Edition* (New York: Twayne Publishers, 1996), 123–124.

KATHLEEN RAINE ON ALCHEMY IN "THE CRYSTAL CABINET"

[Kathleen Raine has authored *Blake and Tradition* and *Golgonooza, City of Imagination: Last Studies in William Blake* and has co-edited a selection of the writings of Thomas Taylor. She also has published several volumes of poetry, including her own. This selection compares a belief in alchemy, a medieval science, to the structure and symbolism in "The Crystal Cabinet".]

There is a more elaborate alchemical myth which Blake seems to have known—again, probably from Vaughan. *The Crystal Cabinet*, an unpublished poem in the Pickering Manuscript, contains recondite alchemical symbolism which Blake may have found in Vaughan's *Aula Lucis*. There is no means of knowing when this poem was written. The existing fair copy was made in about 1803, and it is certainly later than the myth of Enion and Tharmas. But the "shining tent" of *Thel* (1789) suggests that the symbolism may have been known to Blake earlier. The crystal cabinet, the "shining tent, and possibly the "crystal house" of Enitharmon are the alchemical "house of light"—matter—under its usual symbol of water:

> *Matter* . . . is the *House of Light*, here hee (i.e. the light) *dwels* and *builds* for himself, and to speake *Truth*, hee takes up his *lodging* in *sight* of all the *World*. When he first *enters* it, it is a glorious *transparent Roome*, a *Chrystall Castle*, and hee lives like a *Familiar* in *Diamonds*. Hee hath then the *Libertie* to look out at the *Windows*, his *love* is all in his *sight*, I meane that *liquid Venus*, which *lures* him *in*, but this continues not very long. Hee is busie as all *Lovers* are, labours for a more close *Union*, insinuates and

conveyes *himself* into the very substance of his *Love*, so that his *Heat* and *action* stirre up her *moyst Essences*, by whose *meanes* he becomes an *absolute Prisoner*. For at last the *Earth* growes *over him* out of the *water*, so that he is quite shut up in darknesse.

Blake's poem tells of the capturing of a spirit by a "Maiden":

> *The Maiden caught me in the Wild,*
> *Where I was dancing merrily;*
> *She put me into her Cabinet*
> *And Lock'd me up with a golden Key.*

(Is the merry dancer a sunbeam?) "Cabinet" is a word that Vaughan constantly uses in just this sense: "to say that the soul formed the body because she is in the body is to say that the jewel made the cabinet because she is in the cabinet"—and Vaughan in his turn is remembering Paracelsus' coffers in which the senses are generated."

Is the poem a paraphrase of Vaughan's allegory? Many of the images and phrases suggest it: "Now as soone as the Passive spirit attracts the *Anima* . . . then the *aethereall water* in a moment attracts the *Passive spirit*, for this is the first visible Receptacle wherein the *superiour Natures* are *Concentrated*. The Soule being thus confined and imprisoned by lawful] *Magick* in this *Liquid Chrystall*, the Light which is in her streams thorough the Water, and then it is *Lux manifeste visibilis ad oculum*."

Vaughan's "lawfull magick" seems to describe the power of Blake's maiden. But the most striking feature of Blake's poem is the threefold nature of the maiden. The cabinet is of gold, pearl, and crystal; and the maiden of the cabinet is threefold. The outer "cabinet" or body opens into

> *Another Maiden like herself,*
> *Translucent, lovely, shining clear,*
> *Threefold each in the other clos'd—*
> *O, what a pleasant trembling fear!*
>
> *O, what a smile! a threefold Smile*
> *Fill'd me, that like a flame I burn'd;*
> *I bent to Kiss the lovely Maid,*
> *And found a Threefold Kiss return'd.*
>
> *I strove to sieze the inmost Form*
> *With ardor fierce & hands of flame*

This triplicity is an alchemical theme. Vaughan elaborates on the feminine principle, who "below" corresponds to the masculine deity "above," and who is likewise a trinity. He describes the natural triplicity, or "three mothers": "For there are Three above and three beneath, Three—as St. John saith—in Heaven and three on earth. The inferior bear witness of the Superior and are their only proper receptacles. They are signatures and created books wherein we may read the Mysteries of the Supernatural Trinity." Thus the "superior is masculine and eternal, the inferior is feminine and mortal." This feminine trinity Vaughan equates with the three "mothers" of cabalism: "*Emes*, or *Aleph*, *Mem* and *Shin*, are Air, Water and Fire . . . The Heavens were made of the Fire, the Earth was made of the Water . . . and the Ayre proceeded from a middle spirit." Elsewhere he calls these the elementary earth (water), the celestial earth (air), and the spiritual earth (fire). Blake's attempt to grasp the threefold maiden reflects a process commonly described by the alchemists, whose teaching is that the descent into generation takes place in three stages. The fiery soul must initiate the process by wrapping itself in the aerial vestment, and clothed in this airy body, descend into the watery envelope of matter. This process Vaughan describes in his *Anima Magica Abscondita*. A similar triplicity is described by Plutarch (see above, p. 251).

Such, then, is the background of Blake's mysterious little poem, whose simplicity is, as so often, deceptive. The maiden is Vaughan's "liquid Venus," and the soul of light, who has "liberty to look out of the windows," becomes, in Blake, the lover who tells that

> *. . . within it opens into a World*
> *And a little lovely Moony Night.*
>
> *Another England there I saw,*
> *Another London with its Tower*

But in Blake's poem, as in Vaughan's allegory, the "ardor fierce" of the lover leads not to the end he had hoped for but to an incarceration. In Vaughan the earth "grows over" the light; in Blake's poem the spirit becomes "a Weeping Babe":

> *I strove to sieze the inmost Form*
> *With ardor fierce & hands of flame,*
> *But burst the Crystal Cabinet,*

And like a Weeping Babe became—
A weeping Babe upon the wild,
And Weeping Woman pale reclin'd,
And in the outward air again
I fill'd with woes the passing Wind.

The spirit, lured to become the lover of the "liquid Venus" in her crystal house of matter, finds himself snared, taken, and generated.

—Kathleen Raine, *Blake and Tradition*, vol. I (Princeton: Princeton University Press, 1968), 274–276.

"The Marriage of Heaven and Hell"

Blake's "The Marriage of Heaven and Hell" is the longest of his works included in this volume. This free-flowing series of writings begins as a poem; then offers a series of observations about life and brief stories about Biblical prophets, angels and devils; and ends with an almost apocalyptic verse. Blake questions and criticizes Christian beliefs, citing Roman and Greek mythology and the work of Milton to support his arguments. The final line of the work is telling: "For every thing that lives is Holy." Blake is opposed to organized religion, and in "The Marriage of Heaven and Hell" he explains the evolution in his spiritual life to his current beliefs.

The work starts with a section of prose, "The Argument", that describes the taking of a dangerous journey through life whose goal is arrival in Heaven. The holy path is treacherous, and a misstep can be fatal. A "villain" chases the good person off the path and into the wild to find his way among lions, problematizing the journey. In a style typical of Blake's poetic work, such as "The Tyger," the first lines are repeated to end the poem. In "The Marriage of Heaven and Hell" this device is effective.

The next writing describes "a new heaven." It is the first Easter Sunday. Emmanuel Swedenborg, the Swedish scientist and theologian who founded the Church of the New Jerusalem, is the angel guarding the tomb of Christ. His writings are compared to the shroud of linen that covered Christ in death. Blake makes his views very clear: that humankind needs Heaven and Hell because without choice and opposites mankind would have no reason to evolve:

Without Contraries is no progression. Attraction and Repulsion, Reason and Energy, Love and Hate are necessary to Human existence.

From these contraries spring what the religious call Good & Evil. Good is the passive that obeys Reason. Evil is the active springing from Energy.

Good is Heaven. Evil is Hell.

The next segment criticizes the Bible and points out its errors. Simply put: Man has a body and a soul; energy is evil; reason is good. The body craves energy, which is evil. Blake criticizes the Bible for claiming that God will punish man for "following his Energies". Blake's truth is that the body and soul cannot be separated, that energy is life and reason surrounds energy. Instead of "energy" as man's temptation and ultimate downfall, then, it is his eternal delight. Blake cites Milton's *Paradise Lost* as an example of the result of desire denied.

At this point in the work, Blake breaks from arguing his theories on humankind and God to recount fables. The first of these "Memorable Fancies" takes Blake to Hell. There, he is among "Genius; which to the Angels look like torment and insanity." He uses the story as a segue to his "Proverbs of Hell", a series of maxims about life such as

"A wholsom food is caught without a net or trap"

"Prisons are built with stones of Law, Brothels with bricks of Religion."

"The fox condemns the trap, not himself."

"The bird a nest, the spider a web, man friendship"

"The best wine is the oldest, the best water the newest."

The next segment discusses the gods of ancient Greece and Rome. There, poets named the deities and ascribed to them characteristics of nature. The people in these times prayed and sacrificed to gods created by writers. This leads to the second "Memorable Fancy"; this time, Blake is having a conversation with the prophets Isaiah and Ezekiel. In this fictional tale, the Prophets say they made up the God of the Jews—a divinity different from the gods of other countries. Isaiah and Ezekiel told Blake in this fantasy that the hardships they suffered were similar to what poets in ancient Greece and Rome and American Indians did for their art and beliefs.

When the dream ends, Blake predicts that the world will be destroyed by fire six thousand years after its creation. The flames will purify all, and all will live forever. He then says it is his mission to clarify the myth that man's body and soul are separate. He will do this by printing his word in the "infernal method"; and this he did do, publishing his own works by engraving on copper plates in a very labor-intensive and time-consuming process that prevented his publishing as many books as he might have done through more conventional methods. In any case, Blake compares his form of printing to Hell: the flames of Hell melt away the superficial to show that all is infinite.

A theme of printing forms a bridge to the next "Memorable Fancy": a trip to Hell's printing house. There dragons, a viper, an eagle, and lions take books from their creation, dress them up, build them up, and then put them in libraries. It is not the most positive description of the industry.

Blake now gets back to the "contraries" mentioned earlier in the work. He contends that there are only two kinds of people, the Prolific and the Devouring, and that these opposites are both inimical to each other and necessary—for if they were reconciled mankind would cease to exist. Blake accuses religion of trying to unite these opposites and explains that even Jesus Christ came not to unite but to divide.

In the next "Memorable Fancy," Blake debates an angel. The angel warns Blake that the path he is on will lead to damnation and then asks the angel to show him the eternal choices, that he might decide which is the better. The speaker sees the fiery abyss, spiders, and horrific storms that would plague him forever in Hell; he then sees a moonlit river, near which a harp plays in peace. The speaker dresses in a white robe and takes the angel and the writings of Swedenborg to a place between the planet Saturn and the stars. They enter a church, pass through the Bible, and enter a pit. Here they find monkeys, chained up and scratching each other. The monkeys pretend to care for each other, then devour their own. The angel is upset by what he has seen. Blake ends the vision by telling the angel that attempts at the religious conversion of others are futile.

In "Opposition Is True Friendship," Blake attacks Swedenborg. He criticizes the theologian's writings as offering no new insights into religion, only old lies. He says Swedenborg's approach is one-sided, dealing only with angels and not with devils. With no "contraries" in his professed faith, Blake claims, he condemns humankind.

The next "Memorable Fancy" portrays Blake as witness to a discussion between an angel and a devil. The devil describes the worship of God as the appreciation of God's gifts in other people; if one is jealous of another's gifts, by the devil's reasoning, then one does not love God. The angel replies that God is visible in Jesus Christ and Christ gave his blessing to the Ten Commandments. The devil retorts that Jesus did not always follow the Ten Commandments or any other tenet of Judaism. The angel then turns into the prophet Elijah; Blake calls the angel a devil, and they read the Bible together.

As we near the end of "The Marriage of Heaven and Hell", the work takes on an almost apocalyptic tone. "A Song of Liberty" offers a violent description of the end, painting England as a victim of a fiery destruction and military defeat. Ultimately, the King cries out, "The Empire is no more!" The "chorus" that follows foreshadows the end of the Church. The final line—"For every thing that lives is Holy"—reflects Blake's own beliefs. While his spiritual life exceeded the boundaries of established spirituality, the Church filled the necessary function of opposition: "Without contraries there is no progression."

"The Marriage of Heaven and Hell"

JOSEPH ANTHONY WITTREICH JR. ON PARODY OF RELIGIOUS WRITINGS

[Joseph Anthony Wittreich Jr. taught at the University of Wisconsin and co-edited *Blake's Sublime Allegory*. He also wrote *Nineteenth-Century Accounts of William Blake* and the essay "Painted Prophecies: The Tradition of Blake's Illuminated Books". This essay compares "The Marriage of Heaven and Hell" to the Bible's Book of Revelation and Blake's interpretation to those of Milton and Swedenborg.]

Swedenborg had announced a "new heaven" in 1757, but as Blake looks around himself he discovers that Swedenborg's "heaven" is "the Eternal Hell revive[d]," that Swedenborg is, by his own definition, the devil in that hell (*MHH* 3: 34). In *The Apocalypse Revealed*, Swedenborg distinguishes between the hell called "the Devil," by which he means the hell created by those "who are in the love of self," and the hell called "Satan," by which he means the hell created by those who live by "falsities" and "who are in the pride of their own intelligence."[20] Swedenborg begins *The Apocalypse Revealed* with a proclamation: "There are many who labored in the explanation of the *Apocalypse*; but, as the spiritual sense of the Word had been hitherto unknown they could not see the arcana which he concealed therein. for the spiritual sense alone discloses these." Then he makes a pronouncement: *I* am the visionary with "a particular enlightenment" and will now reveal the Book of Revelation.[21] From Blake's viewpoint, Swedenborg "conciev'd himself as much wiser" than be really was. Swedenborg "shews the folly of churches, & exposes hypocrites, till he imagines that all are religious, & himself the single one on earth that ever broke a net." However, this is the "plain fact," says Blake: "Swedenborg has not written one new truth: Now hear another: he has written all the old falsehoods" (*MHH* 21–22; 41–42). *The Marriage of Heaven and Hell* is structured around the opposition between the true and false prophet represented in the satire by Milton and Swedenborg respectively. Like Newton, Swedenborg tried to reduce the spiritual sense, the sublime allegory, of Revelation to corporeal understanding and thereby perverted true religion into a corrupt orthodoxy. Like Milton, Blake preserves the visionary dimension of prophecy, even if doing so requires transforming all the Lord's people into prophets. Rather than perverting sublime allegory into falsehood, Blake would convert an entire civilization into a nation of visionaries. This Newton refused to do and Swedenborg failed to do, both of them by bruising Saint John's minute articulations, and Newton by denying that God ever designed to make people into prophets.[22]

Even so, if Newton and Swedenborg were seen by Blake, on occasion, as types of the false prophet, they were also seen by him, on other occasions, in the posture of the redeemed man. Both Newton and Swedenborg articulated conceptions of prophecy compatible with Blake's own, which explains why in *Milton* Swedenborg is represented as "strongest of men" (22: 50) and why in *Jerusalem* Newton rides a chariot when, "at the clangor of the Arrows of intellect," the apocalypse occurs (98: 7). Precisely because Newton was bound to his own religious culture, he understood that the Book of Daniel and the Book of Revelation were related not only to one another but to all other scriptural prophecies, "so that all of them together make but one complete Prophecy" that "consists of two parts, an introductory Prophecy, and an Interpretation thereof."[23] Each prophet is both creator of his visions and interpreter of them; and every subsequent prophet repeats the pattern but, in the process, becomes an interpreter both of his own visions and of the vision of his predecessors. Behind Newton's understanding is the perception that the Apocalypse subsumes all previous prophetic structures. The Apocalypse is simultaneously an interpretation and a prophecy; by way of repeating all previous prophecies it comments on them, but it also introduces a series of seven new visions, each of which interprets the one it supersedes until in the final vision all things burst into clarity. Swedenborg reveals exactly this understanding when he depicts chapter 22 of Revelation as both in individual vision and a revelation of the total meaning of the Apocalypse.

From Newton and Swedenborg incidentally and from Spenser and Milton quite centrally, Blake took his prophetic stance; and from them all he learned that prophecy had a structure, which epic poetry could appropriate and accommodate. Austin Farrer has observed quite perceptively that in composing the Book of Revelation "St. John was making a new form of literature," but he concludes quite mistakenly that John "had no successor."[24] In Blake's epics, conventional structures are subdued, though not fully eliminated, and the living form of Revelation prophecy imparts the "new" epic structure. Blake's epics turn to Saint John, the last great prophet in Scripture, and to John Milton, the last great prophet in the epic mode; and then they turn, for their structural model, to the culminating vision of each prophet: Milton's vision of paradise regained and John's of apocalypse. In those prophecies, "the summe of Religion is shewed," and it is Blake's task to reveal the essence of those visions, which commentators on Revelation understood as "allegories," penetrable by only the initiated, and which eighteenth-century commentators on Milton seemed not to have understood at all.[25]

NOTES

20. Translated by John Whitehead (New York: Swedenborg Foundation, 1931), I, 113.

21. Ibid., p. iii.

22. See Newton, *Observations*, esp. pp. 251–252, where he says that "the folly of Interpreters" has been to speak "as if God designed to make them Prophets," and then argues that "the design of God was much otherwise."

23. Ibid., p. 254.

24. *A Rebirth of Images: The Making of St. John's Apocalypse* (London: Dacre Press, 1919), p. 305.

25. See Hugh Broughton, *A Revelation of the Holy Apocalypse* ([London], 1610), and my Introduction to *Milton's "Paradise Regained": Two Eighteenth-Century Critiques by Richard Meadowcoart and Charles Dunster* (Gainesville, Fla.: Scholars' Facsimiles and Reprints, 1971).

> —Joseph Anthony Wittreich Jr., "Opening the Seals: Blake's Epics and the Milton Tradition," *Blake's Sublime Allegory*, ed. Stuart Curran and Joseph Anthony Wittreich (Madison: The University of Wisconsin Press, 1973), 29–32.

[Max Plowman wrote *An Introduction to the Study of Blake*
in 1927. In this excerpt, Plowman discusses Blake's Heaven
and Hell as representations of man's hopes and fears.]

Blake suddenly saw these two great contraries as complementary. So
he joined them in holy wedlock and wrote *The Marriage of Heaven
and Hell*. He solved the mystery in himself. Heaven, the realm of
Hope, lay before him. Hell, the region of Fear, lay behind. Vision
was the synchronization of the two. The meeting of hope and fear
was vision, and vision was the perception of identity itself.

The spiritual life descended and was from Heaven. The
instinctive life ascended and was from Hell. As the plant had its
roots in the ground while its shoots aspired towards the sky, so man,
rooted in Hell, aspired to Heaven and flowered upon Earth. Life
instead of being, as the Churches taught, the opportunity for
exercising moral virtue or goodness, and thus showing that man was
one with the Divine Essence, was the means by which man achieved
conscious individual identity, which identity had nothing to do with
good or evil, being an eternal reality awaiting human recognition.
This Principle of identity held good for all things. Sheep and goats,
angels and devils, good men and evil men, cunning and courageous,
prolific and devourers—all were necessary to human existence, for
Without contraries human life was unthinkable. Mortality was not
the opportunity for man's pathetic effort towards eternal sameness,
but was immortality made visible: distinction and difference
revealed so that every living thing might exhibit its eternal form, and
by showing its eternal form reveal its individual holiness.

Thus at one bound Blake released himself from the toils of
morality and surpassed not only Swedenborg but his old friend the
moralist Lavater. Henceforth Good and Evil ceased to be the
essential differences; the essential differences lay deeper and were
not to be resisted, being as necessary to human life as the contrary
acts of respiration were to the body.

For a moment Blake rejoiced in the sense of freedom that always
ensues when we have put behind us restraints not of our own
making, and all restraint seems to be the work of the devil. But of

course Blake had not solved the insoluble problem of duality: he had only raised the standard. The moment we cease to conform to external discipline, in that moment life imposes upon us the necessity of conforming to a far more rigorous discipline—the self-discipline upon which true form depends. Blake passed from the discipline of good and evil to the far more rigorous discipline of imaginative or unimaginative life, and having written the enfranchising *Marriage of Heaven and Hell*, he was soon to find, in tears of repentance, that the very means whereby we achieve spiritual enfranchisement quickly turns to pride unless we pass from vision to vision. God made duality that man might know the supreme joy of balance in the ecstasy of creation; but when vision fades and we eat in pride the fruits of vision, fancying that we have attained, we turn our joy to sorrow. In his moment of insight Blake enfranchised the human body as a part of the human soul; but unless I misinterpret the tears of Urizen in the Fifth Night of *Vala*, the body, in Blake's idea, assumed a pride in its own glory during the years that intervened, and taught Blake that Gods may "combine against Man setting their dominion above The Human Form Divine", and that none is so ready to do this as a rightly-enfranchised instinct.

But now Blake saw very clearly what has since been demonstrated psychologically, that the repression of energy only changes its shape.

How did this discovery appear in the light of Christian dogma?

The Christianity that was based upon the Ten Commandments appeared to exist chiefly to exercise this restraint upon human instinct. It put division between the soul and body and by this putting asunder attempted to frustrate the essential purpose of mortal life which was the manifestation of the soul in form. It separated human life from the continuous life of Eternity by making moral perfection, which was only possible to God as essence, the ideal of human life; the true ideal being the complete revelation of individual identity. In consequence it necessarily destroyed the whole purpose of incarnation. God was removed from earth and transplanted to the abstract heaven, and Jesus, instead of being the Incarnate Word, became merely an ideal historical character.

Blake regarded the Christianity of his day as the spiritual atavism Jesus came to destroy. It was the worship of God as light, a worship which Blake indicates in "The Little Black Boy" as natural and right to man in the childhood of the race, but atavistic and wrong to those who lived in the imaginative manhood of the race. The Divine Image a human form displayed. Even the Little Black Boy, living in the childhood of the race as he is, learns that he is put on earth a little space not only that he may learn to bear the beams of love, but that when he has done this, it may be for the express purpose of shading, his white brother: of being "like him" and thus discovering the Divine Image in a human form.

Blake saw the crux of the whole matter lay in the denial of spiritual purpose to instinctive life. So *The Marriage* resolves itself into a justification of instinct. Not the restraint, but the imaginative redemption of instinct is the purpose of experience; for when this is complete, not only will the five senses appear as "inlets of soul", but the cherub with his flaming sword will leave his guard at the Tree of Life and everything will appear as it is, infinite and holy. Everything that lives is holy, for everything possesses within itself its own sacred law of life, a law that can only be contravened by the imposition of any external law.

—Max Plowman, *An Introduction to the Study of Blake* (New York: Barnes & Noble, 1967), 116–119.

David V. Erdman on Spirituality Versus Society

[David V. Erdman taught at the State University of New York, Stony Brook. He edited *The Poetry and Prose of William Blake* and wrote *Blake: Prophet Against Empire* and the *Concordance of the Works of Blake*; he also served as editor of the publications of the New York Public Library. This essay contrasts the spiritual side of the writing to the work's social implications.]

Blake's *Marriage of Heaven and Hell* mocks those who can accept a spiritual apocalypse but are terrified at a resurrection of the body of society itself. "Energy is the only life and is from the Body," announces the Devil, and it is "Eternal Delight" though the religious may call it Evil (pl. 4). The birth and resurrection of Christ are not the equal and opposite exhalations of the theosophists but progressive stages in the life of man.[8] Blake rejects Swedenborg's "spiritual equilibrium" between good and evil for a theory of spiraling "Contraries" that will account for progress. "Attraction and Repulsion, Reason and Energy, Love and Hate, are necessary to Human existence" (pl. 3). Such *unnecessary* opposites as Bastilles and Moral Codes and the "omissions" due to poverty are merely hindrances that may be scattered abroad "to the four winds as a torn book, & none shall gather the leaves." They "spring from" the *necessary* Contraries but are not to be confused with them. Christ stamped the ten commandments to dust, and history will not return to them except perversely.

Blake is half in jest when he speaks of the "marriage" of Heaven and Hell, for Hell does not exist except as the negative way of looking at Energy, while the Heaven of things-as-they-are is really a delusion like the senile "innocence" of Har and Heva which springs from a denial of the true Heaven of progression. Blake's theory admits of a true or necessary Reason as "the bound or outward circumference of Energy" but leaves it no role in "life" except to be pushed about. Reason is the horizon kept constantly on the move by man's infinite desire. The moment it exerts a will of its own and attempts to restrain desire, it turns into that negative and unnecessary Reason which enforces obedience with dungeons, armies, and priestcraft and which Blake refers to, as "the restrainer" which usurps the place of desire and "governs the unwilling." Tiriel was such a deity, and so is the dismal god of the Archbishop of Paris who can no longer restrain the millions from bursting the bars of Chaos. Blake will soon invent for this sterile god a comic name, Nobodaddy (old daddy Nobody), and an epic name, Urizen, signifying *your reason* (not mine) and the limiting *horizon* (Greek . . ., to bound).[9] The poet's hostility toward this "Governor or Reason" is thoroughly republican or, to the modern mind, socialistic.

Blake's intransigence toward any marriage of convenience between Hell and Heaven appears further in an extended metaphor of conflict which he introduces with a play upon Rousseau's pronouncement that man is born free but is everywhere in chains:

"The Giants who formed this world . . . and now seem to live in it in chains are in truth, the causes of its life & the sources of all activity, but the chains are, the cunning of the weak and tame minds, which have power to resist energy . . . .

"Thus one portion of being, is the Prolific, the other, the Devouring: to the Devourer it seems as if the producer was in his chains, but it is not so, he only takes portions of existence and fancies that the whole."[10]

There is a substratum of reference here to the economic struggle of producer and exploiter or producer and consumer, not without a Mandevillean echo. This struggle is "eternal" in the sense that the producer and consumer even in the false relationships of slavery and commerce are doing what must always be done to sustain life. They are doing it the cheerless way, but even in the freedom of a classless paradise there will always be work and always an audience for the artist-workman, for "the Prolific would cease to be Prolific unless the Devourer as a sea received the excess of his delights."

But Blake's more immediate focus is upon the politics of moral restraint, and he is condemning the conservatism which seeks to confine the oppressed to a passive acceptance of tyranny. "Religion is an endeavour to reconcile" the "two classes of men" who "should be enemies," i.e. to unite the lion and its prey. But "Jesus Christ did not wish to unite but to separate them, as in the Parable of sheep and goats! & he says I came not to send Peace but a Sword."[11] The illusion that energy can be quietly repressed by celestial "wisdom" is exploded by the very fact of revolution. But the fear that revolution means the cessation of all productive relations and of the very means of existence is equally illusory, as Blake proceeds to demonstrate in his fourth "Memorable Fancy."

In this parable Blake and a conservative Angel who is alarmed at his radical "career" undertake to show each other the post-revolutionary future from their respective points of view. The Angel is unwilling to plunge with Blake into the void of the coming century to see whether the Swedenborgian "providence is here also," because what he sees ahead is a "monstrous serpent" with a forehead colored "green & purple" like "a tygers" (17–18). This is what the Revolution looks like to a Tory, and it is symbolic of the fear of Hell which makes him restrain desire. The monster that terrifies him boils up out of the nether deep beside a "cataract of blood mixed with fire" in a manner that prefigures the birth of Orc in *America* which terrifies the King of England.[13] Blake's "friend the Angel" is frightened away. But Blake stands his ground; and since he does not allow himself to be imposed upon by the Angel's "metaphysics," he finds that he ends up, not in the belly of a monster, but sitting peacefully "on a pleasant bank beside a river by moonlight hearing a harper who sung to the harp, & his theme was, The man who never alters his opinion is like standing. water, & breeds reptiles of the mind."[14] The Angel is quite surprised to find that Blake has "escaped" alive. But it is only to the stagnant mind that the energy of revolution appears reptilian and sympathy with rebellion a career leading to a "hot burning dungeon . . . to all eternity" (18).

Blake then "imposes upon" the Tory in his turn, showing this Guildenstern a vision of his future lot, assuming the Swedenborgian Hell to be true. The Tory's clinging to the status quo means that he accepts a phantasmal eternity of cannibalistic relations between Producers and Devourers. A person who assumes that people belong in chains and who scorns the multitude as swinish has nothing to look forward to but a loathly conflict of "monkeys, baboons, & all of that species chain'd by the middle." The Devourers, politician-like, grin and kiss "with seeming fondness" the body of a victim they are devouring limb by limb.[15] The implication seems to be that only those who cannot imagine progressive social change must view the Negations as eternal and assume that human relations will be forever those of joyless slavery.

NOTES

8. To Swedenborg "the delight of the body" is definitely "not heavenly." And his ordered hierarchy of identical but opposite celestial and infernal institutions suggests an essentially static universe. The rich and poor remain rich and poor in Heaven—and presumably in Hell—and the wise Angel, as Swedenborg has been told by Angels of distinction, does not aspire above his rank. *Heaven and Hell*, pars. 35, 375–381, 537.

9. The "reason" in "Urizen" has long been accepted. First to note the "horizon" in it was F. E. Pierce, in 1931. "Nobody's daddy" for "old Nobodaddy" was suggested by John Sampson in 1905.

10. *M.H.H.* 16. A discussion of the "Argument" of *The Marriage*, proper at this point, will be found below (p. 186)—because I originally believed it to be of later vintage; I now see, from the style of lettering, that it cannot have been etched later than 1791.

11. *M.H.H.* 17; cf. *An Answer to the Parson, N.* 103: "Why of the sheep do you not learn peace[?] Because I don't want you to shear my fleece."

In *M.H.H.* Blake is, as he hints, turning back from Swedenborg's sweetness to the "Wrath" of Boehme, who wrote that "unless there were a *contrarium* in God, there would be ... nothing ... merely God ... in a sweet meekness," and that strife "between the fierceness and the meekness" must continue, to eternity. See citations in Stephen Hobhouse, *Selected Mystical Writings of William Law*, New York, 1948, p. 370. For Blake's use of Swedenborg and Boehme in *M.H.H.* see Nurmi, *Blake's Marriage of Heaven and Hell*, pp. 25–59.

12. A suggestion for the passage may be seen in Swedenborg's *True Christian Religion*, par. 74, in which the seer himself is the spokesman of a doctrine that alarms his auditors (they are shocked at how much his stress on "order" seems to *bind* the Omnipotent; he advises those who see a Leviathan in this to hack through it as Alexander did the Gordian knot).

13. The monster is sighted "in the east, distant about, three degrees" or about the distance of Paris from London, as Nurmi points out.

14. *M.H.H.* 19. The harper is doubtless Welsh. In 1791 Blake was employed by Johnson to illustrate a small book by Mary Wollstonecraft. His pictures are faithful to the text with the exception of "The Welsh harper in the hut." Here the story calls for an elderly bard, but Blake has drawn an eager-faced youth.

Note the later ironic comment, in *J*.65, during the long war: " . . . this is no gentle harp . . . nor shadow of a mirtle tree."

15. *M.H.H.* 20. Blake elaborates with Dantesque literalness here Swedenborg's par. 575 on "the gnashing of teeth." He also draws heavily on par. 585 for the cavern entrance to Hell, for an allusion to "stagnant pools," and for a description of the "continual quarrels, enmities, blows, and fightings" in one of the hells. And of course Blake is making the most of Swedenborg's own definition of the fires etc. of Hell as only "appearances."

—David V. Erdman, Blake: *Prophet Against Empire* (Princeton: Princeton University Press, 1969), 178–182.

HAROLD BLOOM ON THE CONTRARIES IN "THE MARRIAGE OF HEAVEN AND HELL"

[Harold Bloom is a Sterling Professor of the Humanities at Yale University. He has written more than 16 books and edited more than 30 anthologies, including *Blake's Apocalypse*, *William Blake's* Songs of Innocence and of Experience, and *Modern Critical Views: William Blake*. In this extract, Bloom considers the various contraries presented in the poem and how they relate to what is human. He also touches on the irony of progress with respect to the cyclical nature of the poem.]

The poem that opens the *Marriage* as "argument" has not been much admired, nor much understood. Rintrah, the angry man in Blake's pantheon, rears and shakes his fires in the burdened air; clouds, hungry with menace, swag on the deep. The poem is a prelude, establishing the tone of prophetic fury that is to run beneath the *Marriage*; the indignation of Rintrah presages the turning over of a cycle.

The poem itself has the cyclic irony of *The Mental Traveller*. The "just man" or "Devil" now rages in the wilds as outcast, having been driven out of "perilous paths" by the "villain" or "Angel." This reversal is simple enough, if it is true reversal, which it is not. The initial complication is provided by the sixth to ninth lines of the poem:

> Roses are planted where thorns grow,
> And on the barren heath
> Sing the honey bees.

Grow, not *grew*; *sing*, not *sang*. We are already involved in the contraries. Cliff is opposed to river, tomb to spring, bleached bones to the red clay of Adam (literal Hebrew meaning). The turning of this cycle converts the meek just man into the prophetic rager, the easeful villain into the serpent sneaking along in mild humility. The triple repetition of "perilous path" compounds the complication. First the just man keeps the perilous path as he moves toward death. But "*then* the perilous path was planted . . . / *Till* the villain left the path of ease, / To walk in perilous paths."

We grasp the point by embracing both contraries, not by reconciling them. There is progression here, but only in the ironic sense of cycle. The path, the way of generation that can only lead to death, is always being planted, the just man is always being driven out; the villain is always usurping the path of life-in-death. When the just man returns from being a voice in the wilderness, he drives the villain back into the nonexistence of "paths of ease." But "just man" and "villain" are very nearly broken down as categories here; the equivocal "Devil" and "Angel" begin tn loom as the *Marriage*'s contraries. The advent of the villain upon the perilous path marks the beginning of a new "heaven," a "mild humility" of angelic restraint. So Blake leaves his argument and plunges into his satiric nuptial Song:

> As a new heaven is begun and it is now thirty-three years since its advent, the Eternal Hell revives.

Swedenborg, writing in his *True Christian Religion*, had placed the Last Judgment in the spiritual world in 1757, the year of Blake's birth. In 1758 Swedenborg published *his* vision of judgment, *Heaven and Hell*. Now, writing in 1790, at the Christological age of thirty-three, Blake celebrates in himself the reviving of the Eternal Hell, the voice of desire and rebellion crying aloud in desert places against the institution of a new divine restraint, albeit that of the visionary Swedenborg, himself a Devil rolled round by cycle into Angelic category.

Before the *Marriage* moves into diabolical gear, Blake states the law of his dialectic:

> Without Contraries is no progression. Attraction and Repulsion, Reason and Energy, Love and Hate, are necessary to Human existence.

The key here is *Human*, which is both descriptive and honorific. This is a dialectic without transcendence, in which heaven and hell are to be married but without becoming altogether one flesh or one family. By the "marriage" of contraries Blake means only that we are to cease valuing one contrary above the other in any way. Echoes of Isaiah xxxiv and xxxv crowd through the *Marriage*, and a specific reference to those chapters is given here by Blake. Reading Isaiah in its infernal sense, as he read *Paradise Lost*, Blake can acknowledge its apocalypse as his own. As the imaginative hell revives, the heaven of restraint comes down.

> And all the host of heaven shall be dissolved, and the heavens shall be rolled together as a scroll: and all their host shall fall down. (Isaiah xxxiv.4) (. . .)

Therefore, the contraries, when next stated in the famous "Voice of the Devil" passage, have ceased strictly to be contraries. Blake's lower or earthly paradise, Beulah Land, is a state of being or place where contraries are equally true, but the *Marriage* is written out of the state of Generation, our world in its everyday aspect, where progression is necessary. Christian dualism is therefore a negation, hindrance, not action, and is cast out beyond the balance of contraries. Blake does not build truth by dialectic, being neither a rational mystic like Plato nor a mystic rationalist like Hegel. Nothing eternal abides behind forms for Blake; he seeks reality in appearances, though he rejects appearance as it is perceived by the lowest-common-denominator kind of observer. Between the cloven fiction of St. Paul's mind–body split and the emotionalism of the celebrator of a state of nature exists the complex apocalyptic humanism of the *Marriage*, denying metaphysics, accepting the hard given of this world, but only insofar as this appearance is altogether human.

Here it has been too easy to mistake Blake for Nietzsche, for D. H. Lawrence, for Yeats, for whatever heroic vitalist you happen most to admire. The *Marriage* preaches the risen body breaking bounds, exploding upward into psychic abundance. But here Blake is as earnest as Lawrence, and will not tolerate the vision of recurrence, as Nietzsche and Yeats do. The altogether human escapes cycle, evades irony, cannot be categorized discursively. But Blake is unlike Lawrence, even where they touch. The Angel teaches light without heat, the vitalist—or Devil—heat without light; Blake wants both, hence the marriage of contraries. (. . .)

In crude terms, the problem is where the stuff of life comes from; where does Reason, divinity of the "Angels," obtain the substance that it binds and orders, the energy that it restrains? By stealing it from the *Urgund* of the abyss, is Blake's diabolic answer. We are almost in the scheme of *The Four Zoas*: the Messiah *fell*, stole the stuff of creativity, and formed "heaven." One contrary is here as true as another: this history has been adopted by both parties. One party, come again to dominance among us, now condemns Blake as a persuasive misreader of *Paradise Lost*. When, in another turn of the critical wheel, we go back to reading *Paradise Lost* in its infernal or poetic sense, as Blake, Shelley, and a host of nineteenth-century poets and scholars did, we will have to condemn a generation of critical dogmatists for not having understood the place of dialectic in literary analysis.

The "Memorable Fancies," brilliant exercises in satire and humanism, form the bulk of the *Marriage*, and tend to evade Blake's own dialectic, being, as they are, assaults, furious and funny, on Angelic culpability. The dialectic of the *Marriage* receives its definitive statement once more in the work, in the opposition of the Prolific and the Devouring. If one grasps that complex passage, one is fortified to move frontally against the most formidable and properly most famous section of the *Marriage*, the "Proverbs of Hell," where dialectic and rhetoric come together combatively in what could be judged the most brilliant aphorisms written in English, seventy gnomic reflections and admonitions on the theme of diabolic vision.

—Harold Bloom, *The Ringers in th eTower: Studies in Romanntic Tradition* (Chicago: University of Chicago Press, 1971), 56–60.

W.J.T. MITCHELL ON THE MARRIAGE OF IMAGES AND WORDS

[W.J.T. Mitchell is the Gaylord Distinguished Service Professor of Art and Literature at the University of Chicago. His publications include *Blake's Composite Art, Picture Theory*, and the essays "Visible Language: Blake's Wond'rous Art of Writing" and "Metamorphoses of the Vortex: Hogarth, Turner and Blake". In this writing, Mitchell explains how the artwork accompanying "The Marriage of Heaven and Hell" complements the combination of contraries.]

It is important to remember the adjective "apparent" when talking about the discrepancies between Blake's designs and text, however, for if we are correct, the most disparate pictorial and verbal structures must conceal a subtle identity of significance. The title page of *The Marriage of Heaven and Hell* {3} exemplifies the way in which the apparent unrelatedness of content in design and text belies the close affinities of formal arrangement. A pair of nudes embrace in a subterranean scene at the bottom of the page, the one on the left emerging from flames, the one on the right from clouds. The top of the page is framed by a pair of trees, between which are two sets of human figures. No scene in the poem corresponds to this picture,[17] and yet it is a perfect representation of the poem's theme, the marriage of contraries:

Without Contraries is no progression. Attraction and Repulsion, Reason and Energy, Love and Hate, are necessary to Human Existence.

From these contraries spring what the religious call Good & Evil. Good is the passive that obeys Reason. Evil is the active springing from Energy.

Good is Heaven. Evil is Hell. (*MHH* 3)

Every aspect of the composition is deployed to present this vision of contraries: flames versus clouds, red versus blue, the aggressive inward thrust of the female flying up from the left versus the receptive outward pose of the figure on the right. At the top, the trees on the left reach their branches across to the right, while the trees on the right recoil into themselves. The couple beneath the trees on the left walk hand in hand toward the right. The couple on the right face away, and are separated, one kneeling, the other lying on the ground. This last detail suggests that the composition is not simply a visual blending of contraries, but also a statement about their relative value. The active side presents a harmonious vision of the sexes; the passive, an inharmonious division, in which the male seems to be trying to woo the female from her indifference by playing on a musical instrument.[18] This tipping of the balance in favor of the "Devil's Party" is accentuated by the direction of movement that pervades the whole design. If we were simply to have a balanced presentation of contraries such as the text suggests, we would expect a simple symmetrical arrangement, with a vertical axis down the center. But, in fact, the whole kinesis of the composition, accentuated by the flying nudes in the center, produces an axis which goes from the lower left corner to the upper right. If one were to draw vectors indicating the probable course of the figures in the center of the design, the result would be [a] diagonal axis.

This tilting of the symmetry of the contraries, is, of course, exactly what happens to the theme of the *Marriage* as Blake treats it. Although the contraries are theoretically equal, Blake has all his fun by identifying himself with the side of the devils. The poem is not simply a self-contained dialectic; it is a dialogue with Blake's own time, and he felt that the "Angels" already had plenty of spokesmen, such as Swedenborg and the apologists for traditional religion and morality. At his particular historical moment, Blake felt that the axis needed to be tilted in favor of energy. Hence, all the good lines in the work and the advantageous pictorial treatments are reserved for the representatives of Hell. But the style of lettering in the title page returns us to the theoretical equality which Blake sees between the contraries. Both "Heaven" and "Hell" are printed in rather stark block letters; the flamboyant, energetic style of free-flowing lines and swirls is reserved for the key term in the poem, "Marriage."

Blake's departure from the literalist implications of *ut pictura poesis* was not, however, simply confined to the avoidance, in his own work, of mere illustration. The doctrine also had implications for the nature of poetry and painting in general, apart from their employment in a composite form like the illustrated book. The concept of the ideal unity of the arts was used to encourage, on the one hand, "painterly," descriptive poetry like Thomson's, and on the other, "poetical," literary painting like Hogarth's. Poetry was to become pictorial by evoking a flood of images which could be reconstituted in the reader's mind into a detailed scene. Painting was to become poetical by imitating a significant action, with beginning, middle, and end.[19] not just a fleeting moment, and by representing not only the surfaces of things but also the interior passions and characters of men. Each art was expected to transcend its temporal or spatial limitation by moving toward the condition of its sister.

NOTES

17. It has been suggested by John E. Grant that the title page "illustrates" the text of *MHH* 24, which describes the dialogue of an angel and devil, and the conversion of the former into the latter. A considerable number of qualifications would have to accompany this view of the relationship: 1) the textual devil and angel are males, while the pictured figures are female; 2) the text describes a conversation followed by a self-immolation, while the design depicts a sexual encounter; 3) the other details of the design do not seem to refer to the text of plate 24. An accurate understanding of the relationship between the design and any textual echoes of its details must take into account, it seems to me, the complex transformations involved in transposing the elements of one to the other. One could argue, for instance, that self-immolation and sexuality are a kind of natural metaphor, and certainly a very Blakean one; yet this would still only scratch the surface of the complex metaphorical layers that would be involved in any equation of *MHH* 1 with *MHH* 24.

J.E.G.: I agree that some of these reservations need to be borne in mind lest one assume, as Damon does, that the episode depicted is intended as an "illustration" in the sense of a literal depiction of the last Memorable Fancy. The hazards of descriptive generalizations based on a single copy, however, need also to be guarded against: the round buttocks and long hair on the figure at the left in copy F (Blake Trust facsimile) make the figure seem female, the more svelte buttocks in copy H (Dent facsimile) could easily be those of a male; hair length is not a safe guide; and Blake often chose not to depict the genitalia of indubitably male figures. One could argue that the pictured "Devil" and "Angel" are both androgynes, but it seems simplest to treat them as male and female respectively, as I have done in my discussion of the page in "Two Flowers in the Garden of Experience," in Rosenfeld, *Essays for Damon*, 363–364. For one thing, the word "Marriage" in the title and these embracing figures on the same page (though the page contains other details, since it is designed for viewers, not just readers) require readers to concern themselves with implications that make sense of the conversion of the Angel at the end of the poem. This conversion is described as his encountering "a Devil in a flame of fire" (cf. the left-hand figure in flames in the title page) and, from where he sits "on a cloud" (cf. the right-hand figure), stretching "out his arms embracing the flame of fire"—upon which "he was consumed and arose as Elijah," who, we are reminded later, "comprehends all the Prophetic Characters" (*VLJ* 83). To summarize this as "self-immolation" is to ignore the transparent and traditional sexual symbolism and to forget there was a Devil in this flame. Were not Blake's title and title page designed to make the human presence of a long-haired Devil in the flame embarrassingly obvious to angelic readers? One must, so to speak, take a Black Panther to lunch before he is fit to enter the kingdom of prophecy.

Those who find anything but the expression of this principle anachronistic are invited to observe several facts. The first is that in copy F, the Blake Trust facsimile, the figure at the right is colored dark brown, quite dark enough to be counted as "black" either in the eighteenth century or now, especially when it is contrasted with the very pinkish "white" figure at the left. It would be more convenient for the reader if this color symbolism were reversed so that the infernal character were black, but the viewer will find the further ironies of the actual coloration both intelligible and satisfying. He will also observe that Blake did not employ this color symbolism in most versions of the book, but understand that this does not negate the significance in copies where he did so.

If a contemporary racist, such as Gillray, had seen the title page of copy F, he might have concluded that Blake was advocating miscegenation. But two other considerations will assist the appreciation of Blake's point in all versions of this design. Although the relationships indicated in the background are more intimate, the central consummation depicted is clearly no more than a kiss. In the text of *MHH* 24 Blake neglects to mention the human form in the flame embraced by the Angel—and thus prevents the conversion of angelic character from seeming easy. In the introduction to this section, in plate 22, Blake declares that the writings of Dante are infinitely more informative than those of the angelic Swedenborg; perhaps Blake had already read that episode in the *Purgatorio* where Dante, like all pilgrims to eternity, must pass through the circumambient fire of love to return, like Adam into paradise, to where Beatrice is.

There have been many accounts of what *The Marriage of Heaven and Hell* is about. I say it is about the education of the Prophetic Character. Blake is committed to showing how much pain and dislocation such an education demands. Though he was honest about the magnitude of the task, he was glad to join with Moses and Milton in praying that all the Lord's people become prophets.

18. The reclining figure is clearly a woman in copy C (Morgan Library) and in copy D and the Trianon Press facsimile of this copy; the instrument held by the kneeling figure is only suggestively etched—probably a flute or shepherd's pipe, or it could be a lyre.

19. See ch. 9, "The Unity of Action," in Lee's "'Ut Pictura Poesis.'"

> —W.J.T. Mitchell, "Blake's Composite Art," *Blake's Visionary Forms Dramatic*, ed. David V. Erdman and John E. Grant (Princeton: Princeton University Press, 1970), 63–66.

ALGERNON CHARLES SWINBURNE ON MUSIC AND MEANING

[Algernon Charles Swinburne, an influential 19th-century poet and literary critic, was a great admirer of Blake. His essays were published in *The Complete Works of A.C. Swinburne*. In this excerpt, Swinburne, praising the musical quality of the prose, calls the poem Blake's greatest work and comments on Blake's message.]

In 1790 Blake produced the greatest of all his books; a work indeed which we rank as about the greatest produced by the eighteenth century in the line of high poetry and spiritual speculation. The *Marriage of Heaven and Hell* gives us the high-water mark of his intellect. None of his lyrical writings show the same sustained strength and radiance of mind; none of his other works in verse or prose give more than a hint here and a trace there of the same harmonious and humorous power, of the same choice of eloquent words, the same noble command and liberal music of thought; small things he could often do perfectly, and great things often imperfectly; here for once he has written a book as perfect as his most faultless song, as great as his most imperfect rhapsody. His fire of spirit fills it from end to end; but never deforms the body, never singes the surface of the work, as too often in the still noble books of his later life. Across the flicker of flame, under the roll and roar of water, which seems to flash and resound throughout the poem, a stately music, shrill now as laughter and now again sonorous as a psalm, is audible through shifting notes and fitful metres of sound. The book swarms with heresies and eccentricities; every sentence bristles with some paradox, every page seethes with blind foam and surf of stormy doctrine; the humour is of that fierce grave sort, whose cool insanity of manner is more horrible and more obscure to the Philistine than any sharp edge of burlesque or glitter of irony; it is huge, swift, inexplicable; hardly laughable through its enormity of laughter, hardly significant through its condensation of meaning; but as true and thoughtful as the greatest humourist's. The variety and audacity of thoughts and words are incomparable: not less so their fervour and beauty. 'No bird soars too high if he soars with his own wings.' This proverb might serve as a motto to the book: it is one of many 'Proverbs of Hell'.

—Algernon Charles Swinburne, "Critics on Blake: 1803–1941," *Critics on Blake: Readings in Literary Criticism*, ed. Judith O'Neill (Coral Gables: University of Miami Press, 1970), 21–22.

MARK BRACHER ON HOW "THE MARRIAGE OF HEAVEN AND HELL" CHANGES THE READER

[Mark Bracher is Assistant Professor of English and Associate Director of the Center for Literature and Psychoanalysis at Kent State University. His published work includes *Being Form'd: Thinking Through Blake's Milton* and several articles on Blake and psychoanalytic approaches to reading. In this essay, Bracher explores the impact of Blake's writing on his readers.]

In the past half century Blakeans have made considerable progress in comprehending these difficult and often intractable elements, but relatively few attempts have been made to understand how these elements might work to effect that psychological transformation of the reader that Blake so expressly desired. Though many commentators refer to "the reader" in discussing Blake's poetry, their attention tends to focus on the reader's immediate (and transient) response, rather than on more substantial and permanent transformations that the poetry might promote. The only long-term changes that are even considered are alterations of the reader's philosophical ideas—i.e., the reader's "sacred code" (*MHH* 4)—and even here, little is said about how such alteration is elicited, or about its significance for the reader's total psychic economy. This omission is of course easily explained by the fact that criticism has until recently lacked the tools to carry out such an investigation: it has had no clear notion of how literature might promote psychological transformation. Now, however, although a comprehensive theory of such transformation has still not been developed, advances in our understanding of the role language plays in the psychic economy make it possible to begin to analyze and assess Blake's poetry in the terms in which he himself clearly viewed it: as a force capable of promoting change in the reader. (. . .)

Such, at least, is one path our interpretation can take through the discourse of the Prolific and the Devouring. In the memorable fancy that follows (*MHH* 17–20), we have little choice: we are thrust upon this path by a powerful interpellation. Here we are forced to experience, with the speaker, the power of language from both sides: that of being interpellated, imposed upon, castrated by it, and that of using it to express one's own subjective realities and force others to recognize them. In the first episode of the fancy, we see the "eternal lot" of the speaker as that lot is determined by the angel's orthodox code. We are made to experience a series of repulsive images, which, however, disappear as soon as the angel leaves, to be replaced by a pleasant scene. What we thus experience is the fact that any given code automatically interpellates a hearer into a particular position that entails a proximity with certain specific images and fantasies, together with their attendant anxieties and desires. This is stated quite explicitly when the speaker declares to the angel: "All that we saw was owing to your metaphysics"—i.e., to the fundamental signifying chains of the angel's code. In the second episode of the fancy, we experience the same fact, only this time from the other position, that of phallic potency, as the speaker, with whom we have identified, shows the angel the angel's lot. In this fancy we thus experience in both the imaginary and the symbolic registers the power of the symbolic code to determine imaginary, subjective experience—i.e., the code's phallic/castrating power.

After a condemnation of logic and systematic reasoning—of remaining within a particular symbolic system, not conversing with devils (desire) and thus opening up the symbolic to the imaginary— we encounter the poem's final memorable fancy, in which we are led through an experience of how our desire can express itself even when we are within an alienating code that denies recognition to our desire. This phallic potency resides in interpretation, and we experience interpretation here in what is perhaps its most potent form—a proto-deconstructive reading. One key term of the orthodox code, "Jesus," is interpreted in such a way as to contradict another key term, the "ten commandments," which the orthodox code places in concord with "Jesus" (as the angel puts it, "Has not Jesus Christ given his sanction to the law of ten commandments?"). In this way, "Jesus," the supreme *point de capiton* of the sacred code, is placed in opposition to other *points de capiton* and, in fact, to codes as such: "Jesus was all virtue, and acted from impulse: not from rules." This interpretation allows recognition not only for particular desires forbidden by the ten commandments, but for all desire whatsoever. Desire, the antithesis of system, is thus inscribed as a radically self-deconstructing element of the symbolic system itself, and desire as such thus acquires being.

Hence, through this final fancy, we experience two ways of overcoming the castrating power of language and regaining phallic potency: we can accept the code but interpret it in such a way that it accommodates our desire (the speaker's strategy), or we can refuse to accept the given code (Jesus' strategy) and thus (implicitly or explicitly) subscribe to an alternative code. Our desire, that is, can gain recognition either through (strong) reading or (strong, poetic) writing. As Blake's speaker indicates at the first ending of *The Marriage*, we can either "read the Bible," the given code, "in its infernal or diabolical sense," or we can write a "Bible of Hell," a new code in which desires are explicitly recognized, legitimized.

As we have seen, it is in such recognition of desire—such a marriage of heaven (the sacred code) and hell (desire)—that Lacanian psychoanalysis locates the efficacy of the psychoanalytic process. By evoking our repressed desires, by providing us with a new code that offers fuller recognition of our desire, and by interpellating us to a position where we must either accept such a code or construct it through interpretation, Blake's poem arouses our faculties to act in such a way as to enact a marriage that constitutes psychological transformation. This process constitutes a marriage of heaven and hell in another sense as well: by eliciting deep fantasies of phallic potency and castration within a metaphysical context, the poem allows our desire to assume more coherent, less conflicting forms, in which a (displaced and sublimated) fulfillment (heaven) is possible even in face of the inescapable reality of castration, or human finitude (hell).

—Mark Bracher, "Rouzing the Faculties: Lacanian Psychoanalysis and the Marriage of Heaven and Hell in the Reader," *Critical Paths: Blake and the Argument of Method*, ed. Dan Miller, Mark Bracher, and Donald Ault (Durham: Duke University Press, 1987), 168.

WORKS BY

William Blake

"Joseph of Arimathea Among the Rocks of Albion" (engraving) (1773)

"The Body of Edward I in his Coffin" (sketch) (1774)

"Edward and Eleanor" (engraving) (1779)

"Penance of Jane Shore in St. Paul's Church" (watercolor) (1779)

"Lear and Cordelia in Prison" (watercolor) (1779)

Exhibition of "The Death of Earl Godwin" at the Royal Academy of Art (1780)

"Glad Day" (drawing) (1780)

Poetical Sketches printed (1783)

"Witch of Endor Raising the Spirit of Samuel" (1783)

"An Allegory of the Bible" (watercolor) (1783)

"The Good Farmer" (1783)

"Three Figures in a Landscape" (1783)

"War" and "A Breach in the City" exhibited at the Royal Academy (1784)

An Island in the Moon (1784)

"Joseph's Brethren Bowing Before Him" (1785)

"Joseph Ordering Simeon to be Bound" (1785)

"Joseph Making Himself known to his Brethren" (1785)

"Shakespeare's *Midsummer Night's Dream*" (watercolor) (1785)

"All Religions Are One" (1788)

"There Is No Natural Religion" (1788)

Sketches for *Tiriel* (1789)

Tiriel (1789)

Songs of Innocence (1789)

The Book of Thel (1789)

"The Beggar's Opera, Act III" (engraving) (1789)

"The House of Death" (1789)

Plates for *Original Stories from Real Life* (Wollstonecraft) (1791)
America (1791)

Plates for *Narrative of a Five Year's Expedition, against the Revolted Negroes of Surinam* (Stedman) (1791–1793, published 1796)

Notebook: lyrics (1791)

The French Revolution (1791, not published)

A Song of Liberty (1792)

"The Penance of Jane Shore in St. Paul's Church" (revised) (1793)

For Children: The Gates of Paradise (1793)

America: A Dream of Thirlaltha (1793)

Visions of the Daughters of Albion (1793)

Prospectus: To the Public (1793)

The Marriage of Heaven and Hell (1794)

The Songs of Experience (published with *The Songs of Innocence*) (1794)

Europe: A Prophecy (1794)

The Book of Urizen (1794)

A Divine Image (1794)

The Book of Los (1795)

The Book of Ahania (1795)

"Christ Appearing to the Apostles After the Resurrection" (watercolor) (1795)

Plates for *Young's Night Thoughts* (Edwards's edition; completed in 1797) (1795)

"God Judging Adam" (engraving) (1795)

"The Elohim Creating Adam" (1795)

"Elijah About to Ascend in the Chariot of Fire" (watercolor) (1795)

"The Good and Evil Angels Struggling for Possession of a Child" (watercolor) (1795)

"Nebuchadnezzar" (watercolor) (1795)

"Lamech and his Two Wives" (watercolor) (1795)

"The Lazar House" (watercolor) (1795)

"Pity" (watercolor) (1795)

"Glad Day" (1795)

"Non Angeli" (1795)

"Sad Angeli" (1795)

"Hecate" / "The Night of Enitharmon's Joy" (watercolor) (1795)

"Newton" (watercolor) (1795)

Illustrates *Leonora* (Burger) (1796)

"Lucifer and the Pope in Hell" (etching) (1796)

Plates for *Thoughts on Outline* (for friend George Cumberland) (1796, begun 1794–1795)

Narrative (Stedman) published (1796)

Vala (1797)

"The Body of Abel Found by Adam and Eve" (watercolor) (1799)

"Bathsheba at the Bath" (tempera) (1799)

"Eve Tempted by the Serpent" (1799)

"The Agony in the Garden" (tempera) (1799)

"Lot and His Daughters" (tempera) (1799)

"Landscape near Felpham" (watercolor) (1800)

Plates for *Little Tom the Sailor* (Hayley) (1800)

"The Death of the Virgin" (watercolor) (1803)

Plates for *Life of William Cowper* (Hayley) (1803)

Plates for *Triumphs of Temper* (Hayley) (1803)

"Pickering" manuscripts (1803)

Milton (1804)

"Ezekiel's Wheels" (1804)

"Goliath Cursing David" (1804)

"The Entombment" (watercolor) (1805)

"Jacob's Dream" (1805)

"God Blessing the Seventh Day" (1805)

"Clothed with the Sun" (1805)

"Satan in his Original Glory" (watercolor) (1805)

"Thou Wast Perfect Till Iniquity Was Found in Thee" (1805)

"David Delivered Out of Many" (watercolor) (1805)

Illustrations for *Paradise Lost* (1807)

"Jacob's Dream" (watercolor) (1808)

"Christ in the Sepulchre, Guarded by Angels" (watercolor) (1808)

"Vision of Judgement" (1808)

"The Angel Rolling Away the Stone From the Sepulchre: The Resurrection" (1808)

"Canterbury Pilgrims" (oil) (1809)

"The Spiritual Form of Pitt Guiding Behemoth" (tempera) (1809)

"The Bard, from Gray" (tempera) (1809)

"The Spiritual Form of Nelson Guiding Leviathan" (tempera) (1809)

"Milton" (engraving) (1809)

"The Whore of Babylon" (engraving) (1809)

Jerusalem (begun 1804) (1810)

"The Great Red Dragon" (watercolor) (1810)

"The Woman Clothed with the Sun" (watercolor) (1810)

Public Address (1810)

"A Vision of the Last Judgement" (1810)

Illustrations for *On the Morning of Christ's Nativity* (Milton) (1815)

Designs for *L'Allegro* (1816)

Designs for *Il Penseroso* (1816)

Hesiod (1817)

"For the Sexes: The Gates of Paradise" (1818)

The Everlasting Gospel (1818)

"Visionary Heads" (1819)

Jerusalem printed (1820)

Woodcuts for *The Pastorals of Virgil* (Thornton) (1820)

"On Homer's Poetry" (1820)

"Old Parr When Young" (1820)

"On Virgil" (1820)

"Mirth and Her Companions" (1820)

"The Laocoon" (1820)

Job series (watercolors) (1821)

The Ghost of Abel (1821)

"Epitome of James Hervey's *Meditations Among the Tombs*"
   (1821)

Designs for *The Pilgrim's Progress* (Bunyan) (1824)

"Moses Placed in the Ark of Bulrushes" (watercolor) (1824)

"Winter" (tempera) (1824)

Dante drawings (1825)

"Virgin & Child (Black Madonna)" (1825)

Job published (1825)

"The Body of Abel Found by Adam and Eve" (tempera) (1826)

"Satan Smiting Job with Sore Boils" (tempera) (1826)

"Ancient of Days" (watercolor) (1826)

William Blake

Abrahams, Cecil Anthony. *William Blake's Fourfold Man.* Bonn: Bouvier, 1978.

Ackroyd, Peter. *Blake.* New York: Alfred A. Knopf, 1996.

Ault, Donald D. *Visionary Physics: Blake's Response to Newton.* Chicago: University of Chicago Press, 1974.

Behrendt, Stephen C. *Reading William Blake.* London: Macmillan, 1992.

Bentley, G.E., Jr. *Blake Records.* Oxford: Clarendon, 1969.

Bloom, Harold. *Blake's Apocalypse: A Study in Poetic Argument.* Ithaca: Cornell University Press, 1970.

———. *The Visionary Company: A Reading of English Romantic Poetry.* Rev. ed. Ithaca: Cornell University Press, 1971.

———, ed. *Modern Critical Views: William Blake.* New York: Chelsea House, 1985.

———, ed. *William Blake's* Songs of Innocence and of Experience. New York: Chelsea House, 1987.

Bronowsji, Jacob. *William Blake and the Age of Revolution.* New York: Harper and Row, 1965.

Cantor, Paul A. *Creature and Creator: Myth-Making and English Romanticism.* Cambridge: Cambridge University Press, 1984.

Cox, Stephen. *Love and Logic: The Evolution of Blake's Thought.* Ann Arbor: University of Michigan Press, 1992.

Crehan, Stewart. *Blake in Context.* Dublin: Gill and Macmillan Humanities Press, 1984.

Curran, Stuart, and Joseph Anthony Wittreich, eds. *Blake's Sublime Allegory: Essays on* The Four Zoas, Milton, Jerusalem. Madison: University of Wisconsin Press, 1973.

Damon, S. Foster. *William Blake: His Philosophy and Symbols.* 1924. Gloucester: Peter Smith, 1958.

Damrosch Jr, Leopold. *Symbol and Truth in Blake's Myth.* Princeton: Princeton University Press, 1980.

Davis, Michael. *William Blake: A New Kind of Man*. Berkeley: University of California Press, 1977.

Erdman, David V. *Blake: Prophet Against Empire*. Princeton, NJ: Princeton University Press, 1969.

Erdman, David V., ed. *The Complete Poetry and Prose of William Blake*. With commentary by Harold Bloom. 1965. Rev. ed. Berkeley: University of California Press, 1988.

Erdman, David V., ed. and Grant, John E., ed. *Blake's Visionary Forms Dramatic*. Princeton: Princeton University Press, 1970.

Ferber, Michael. *The Social Vision of William Blake*. Princeton: Princeton University Press, 1985.

Frye, Northrop. *Blake: A Collection of Critical Essays*. Englewood Cliffs, NJ: Prentice-Hall, 1966.

———. *Fearful Symmetry: A Study of William Blake*. Princeton: Princeton University Press, 1947.

Fuller, David. *Blake's Heroic Argument*. London: Croom Helm, 1988.

Gallant, Christine. *Blake and the Assimilation of Chaos*. Princeton: Princeton University Press, 1978.

Grant, John E., ed. *Discussions of William Blake*. Boston: D.C. Heath and Company, 1961.

Hagstrum, Jean H. *The Romantic Body: Love and Sexuality in Keats, Wordsworth, and Blake*. Knoxville: University of Tennessee Press, 1985.

Harper, George Mills. *The Neoplatonism of William Blake*. Chapel Hill: University of North Carolina Press, 1961.

Hilton, Nelson, ed. *Essential Articles for the Study of William Blake, 1970–1984*. Hamden: Anchor, 1986.

Keynes, Geoffrey. *Blake Studies*. 1949. 2nd ed. Oxford: Clarendon, 1971.

Lindsay, Jack. *William Blake: His Life and Work*. London: Constable, 1978.

Mellor, Anne K. *Blake's Human Form Divine*. Berkeley: University of California Press, 1974.

Miller, Dan, Mark Bracher, and Donald Ault, eds. *Critical Paths: Blake and the Argument of Method*. Durham, N.C.: Duke University Press, 1987.

Murry, John Middleton. *William Blake*. London: Jonathan Cape, 1933.

Nurmi, Martin K. *William Blake*. Kent: Kent State University Press, 1976.

O'Neill, Judith, ed. *Critics on Blake*. Coral Gables: University of Miami Press, 1970.

Ostriker, Alicia. *Vision and Verse in William Blake*. Madison: University of Wisconsin Press, 1965.

Paananen, Victor. *William Blake: Updated Edition*. New York: Twayne, 1996.

Pagliaro, Harold. *Selfhood and Redemption in Blake's Songs*. University Park: Pennsylvania State University Press, 1987.

Paley, Morton D. *Energy and the Imagination: A Study of the Development of Blake's Thought*. Oxford: Clarendon, 1970.

Paley, Morton D., ed. *Twentieth-Century Interpretations of* Songs of Innocence and Experience. Englewood Cliffs, NJ: Prentice-Hall, 1969.

Percival, Milton. *William Blake's Circle of Destiny*. New York: Columbia University Press, 1938.

Phillips, Michael, ed. *Interpreting Blake*. Cambridge: Cambridge University Press, 1978.

Plowman, Max. An Introduction to the Study of Blake. New York: Barnes and Noble, 1967.

Punter, David, ed. *New Casebooks: William Blake*. New York: St. Martin's, 1996.

Raine, Kathleen. *Blake and Tradition*. Princeton: Bollingen Foundation, 1968.

————. *Golgonooza, City of Imagination: Last Studies in William Blake*. Hudson: Lindisfarne Press, 1991.

Rothenberg, Molly Anne. *Rethinking Blake's Textuality*. Columbia: University of Missouri Press, 1993.

Schorer, Mark. *William Blake: The Politics of Vision*. New York: Henry Holt and Company, 1946.

Wagenknecht, David. *Blake's Night: William Blake and the Idea of Pastoral*. Cambridge: Harvard University Press, 1973.

Williams, Nicholas. *Ideology and Utopia in the Poetry of William Blake*. Cambridge: Cambridge University Press, 1998.

ACKNOWLEDGMENTS

"Reading Blake's Lyrics: 'The Tyger'" by Hazard Adams from *Discussions of William Blake* © 1961 by Heath and Company. Reprinted by Permission.

"The Art and Argument of 'The Tyger'" by John E. Grant from *Discussions of William Blake* © 1961 by Heath and Company. Reprinted by Permission.

Selfhood and Redemption in Blake's Songs by Harold Pagliaro © 1987 by The Pennsylvania State University Press. Reprinted by Permission.

"Blake's Revisions of the Tyger" by Martin K. Nurmi from *Twentieth Century Interpretations of Songs of Innocence and of Experience* ©1969 by Prentice Hall. Reprinted by Permission.

Blake in Context by Stewart Crehan © 1984 by Gill and Macmillan Humanities Press. Reprinted by Permission.

"Tyger of Wrath" by Morton D. Paley from *Twentieth Century Interpretations of Songs of Innocence and of Experience* © 1969 by Prentice Hall. Reprinted by Permission.

"The Vision of Innocence" by Martin Price from *Critics on Blake: Readings in Literary Criticism* © 1970 by the University of Miami Press. Reprinted by Permission.

"Infinite London: The Songs of Experience in their Historical Setting" by David V. Erdman from *Critics on Blake: Readings in Literary Criticism* © 1970 by the University of Miami Press. Reprinted by Permission.

"Blake's Cities: Romantic Forms of Urban Renewal" by Kenneth Johnston from *Blake's Visionary Forms Dramatic* © 1970 by Princeton University Press. Reprinted by Permission.

"London" by E.P. Thompson from *Interpreting Blake* © 1978 by Cambridge University Press. Reprinted by Permission.

"Influence and Independence in Blake" by John Beer from *Interpreting Blake* © 1978 by Cambridge University Press. Reprinted by Permission.

Themes and Ideas